S K I L F U L
FIELD
ATHLETICS

— Carl Johnson —

A & C Black · London

First published 1990 by
A & C Black (Publishers) Ltd,
35 Bedford Row, London WC1R 4JH

© Carl Johnson 1990

ISBN 0 7136 5769 3

A CIP catalogue record for this book is available from
the British Library.

Typeset by Latimer Trend & Company Ltd, Plymouth
Printed and bound in Great Britain by
William Clowes Ltd, Beccles and London.

CONTENTS

Acknowledgements

My thanks go to all those hundreds of athletes who permitted me to make mistakes at their expense, and from whom I gained my coaching experience, but especially Julian, Tanya, Emma, Rob, John, Paul, Gillian, Gail, Caroline and Duncan, who gave of their time and ability to assist in the photographic sessions.

I also wish to thank the managers of Gateshead International Stadium and Monkton Stadium, Jarrow, for generous provision of facilities.

Last but not least, I wish to thank my wife Isabel for her help and forbearance through the trauma of turning a worthwhile idea into reality.

Note Throughout the book players are referred to individually as 'he'. This should, of course, be taken to mean 'he or she' where appropriate.

Similarly, in accordance with the IAAF rules, metric-only measurements are given (although in some instances, for example with ratios, imperial forms have had to be used).

Cover photograph courtesy of Sporting Pictures (UK) Ltd. All other photographs courtesy of Action Plus Photographic except for those in Chapter 11.

Line illustrations on pages 12 and 46 by Taurus Graphics.

INTRODUCTION

Track events have an immediacy which makes them easy to follow and to understand, and thus appealing to performer and spectator alike. In contrast, field event competitions are drawn-out affairs in which relative performances and positions become obscured when attention is not concentrated. Thus they tend to hold interest and satisfaction only for the connoisseur.

This is unfortunate, for field events have an appeal which can become all-absorbing for those who are lucky enough to get to know them well, particularly youngsters both at school and in athletics clubs. Many do not get a fair chance to experience field events properly for reasons not of their own choosing, and they are thus unable to form judgements about them. This cannot be right or justifiable.

There are eight field events, comprising four jumping events and four throwing events. The jumping events are high jump, long jump, triple jump (sometimes wrongly referred to as hop, step and jump) and pole vault. The throwing events are shot put, discus throw, javelin throw and hammer throw.

Pole vault and shot put, as their names imply, are a little different from the other disciplines in their groups: the vault is an aided jump, in that the vaulter swings on a pole, while the put is a push and not a throw in the strict sense of the word. In high jump and pole vault, athletes compete for height over a bar (or barrier). All other field events are contests for horizontal distance.

Before 1988, events such as triple jump, hammer and pole vault were considered to be unsuitable for women and girls. However, things are now changing fast in line with the swing during the 1980s towards equality of opportunity for women. This book reflects this trend and actively encourages participation in these three events by women as well as men.

Decathlon (ten disciplines) for men, and heptathlon (seven disciplines) for women are grouped as 'multi' or 'combined' events for all-rounders, involving a mixture of running, jumping and throwing. Despite the fact that running ability and training constitute the major factors determining success or failure, decathlon and heptathlon are traditionally considered field events.

The good teacher/coach will quickly recognise in his charges those qualities which are worth enhancing and those which require modification. It is bad coaching practice to build field event skills in an uncontrolled manner. Thus the training regime of the field eventer must embrace greater technical discipline than that of most track athletes. The sooner the performer accepts such discipline, the better it is for them. It is very easy for careless, insensitive teaching and coaching to run riot as the result of a slavish adherence to either enjoyment, activity or motivation. A modicum of planning can place athlete, technique, enjoyment and motivation in their rightful context, thus achieving a harmonious outcome.

Under such circumstances athletes will develop at rates suitable to themselves, and remain enthusiastic, committed and technically sound. This is the surest base upon which to establish an athletic career, and one on which the athlete may later build to successfully express his own athletic individuality.

THE JUMPS

Most athletes, and many coaches, commit the cardinal sin of paying too much attention to the flight phase of the jump. This is quite wrong since the path followed by a jumper's centre of gravity cannot be changed once he leaves the ground; it is predetermined by the horizontal and vertical forces acting at the moment of take-off. Thus flight techniques only contribute 5 to 10 per cent of the final height or distance attained and teaching, coaching and training should concentrate on the approach and the take-off (particularly the latter). This principle still holds true even in pole vault, which has an aided clearance.

It is important that, whatever the arrangement of the individual aspects of the approach, they should combine to bring the athlete either on to the take-off board, or to the correct take-off spot. This enables him to generate the greatest propulsive force that he is capable of handling and to channel it in the direction best suited to himself.

In long jump, triple jump and pole vault the jumper will only have about one sixth of a second in which to do this. The high jumper will have a few hundredths of a second longer. If the contact time at take-off can be extended by a few milliseconds without loss of previously accumulated force, then a better performance will result. If it cannot, the end product will then be a detrimental one. Increased strength throughout the take-off action will help jumpers to overcome such a deficiency, and to handle the considerable stress which the take-off leg must absorb if they are to channel greater runway forces into the jump.

Beginners, and those working with beginners, will find it most profitable to concentrate on establishing the following aspects of jumping which are common to all four events.

1. **Flex the take-off leg.** One cannot jump high from a straight leg. Having said that, fast approach runs cause the leg to flex automatically, thus the focus of coaching and performance may often have to be completely opposite to that required – that is the emphasis is on keeping the hips high.
2. **Lower the hips.** If the take-off leg is flexed the hips must lower. (It may be easier for the performer to think of the latter rather than concentrate upon what the leg is doing.)
3. **Fix the hips forwards,** directly under the spine, so that the leg forces are transmitted upwards through the spine.
4. **Drive upwards through the hips** or through the top of the head at take-off in order to effectively channel take-off forces and attain essential height.
5. **Punch high with the free limbs** during take-off to efficiently use the take-off forces.
6. **Seek a long take-off,** not a staccato one. This ensures that force is applied for the optimum length of time.

It is not possible to set common principles for the way in which the foot is planted at take-off since this differs according to the event.

During the early stages of learning it is good policy to establish runway discipline. Accuracy is not that vital during the very first stages, although it becomes more so later on. However, a consistent running pattern is very important.

Some people prefer to use an odd number of strides, and others an even number. My own preference is for an approach run composed of an even number, since this enables the jumper to 'toe' the start mark with the take-off foot – easy to do and easy to remember. It is also the most natural option for the pole vaulter, making it perfectly capable of being used as a common principle. From this a seventh principle can be established.

7. Begin an even stride approach run by toeing the start mark with the take-off foot.

The quickest jumpers need the longest runs. Twenty or more running strides are usual for men of international standard, slightly less for women and even less for younger athletes. A useful 'rule of thumb' guide is 12 strides for 12-year-olds, 14 for 14-year-olds and 16 for 16-year-olds. A check-mark placed to encourage a full blooded first stride is useful for absolute novices.

8. Only consistent approach running produces accuracy.

Forcing speed on the runway tends to reduce stride length and bring the athlete short of the correct take-off spot.

Once a consistent approach run has been established, and at the end of each subsequent training session in which modifications to the approach have been made, measure it. This is where a tape measure is useful, although it can be done just as accurately in foot lengths if one is careful, and one's feet are not as easily left at home on competition day! I have to confess to a personal preference for the latter approach.

HIGH JUMP

This event is the preserve of the taller athlete who is also endowed with great natural spring. Sprinting speed, so obviously necessary to long jumping success, is not such an important criterion. Although there are instances of smaller athletes competing successfully in the event, even at international standard, they are the exception rather than the rule.

Safety

The landing area

High jumping is perhaps the most dangerous of all the athletic events, particularly since the advent of the 'Fosbury flop' style of jumping. The 'flop' technique requires special safety provisions and yet because it is so satisfying to do it is popular with both sexes and all ages. The flop is only safe when performed on to a proper, commercially produced, foam landing area or bed. International rules require that such an area measures at least 5 m × 3 m, although some countries recommend 5 m × 2.5 m for younger athletes.

No specifications exist concerning the recommended depth of the landing area. The general principle is that it should be sufficiently deep to prevent jumpers from compressing it to such an extent that they 'bottom' or strike the ground when they land. The density of the foam, the weight of the jumper and the height from which he is falling all have some bearing upon this. A further consideration is that foam degenerates with age, and so ought to be checked annually and replaced when it loses its resilience.

It is vital that the individual units which go together to make the whole bed are securely fastened to one another. Also, these units should be covered with a continuous sheet in order to prevent jumpers from slipping between them.

Sand pits are entirely unsuitable for any form of jump in which the landing is not made on the feet, that is the flop, the 'straddle', and even possibly the 'western roll'. At the same time, foam areas are not particularly suitable for the 'scissors' style of jumping.

The take-off

The key factor in determining safety is an accurately fixed take-off, close to the nearer upright. A take-off from point X in figure 1 will produce a safe landing right in the middle of the area, whereas one from either point Y or point Z cannot guarantee that the area will not be missed completely.

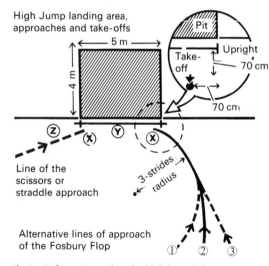

High Jump landing area, approaches and take-offs

5 m

4 m

Pit

Take-off

Upright

70 cm

70 cm

Z X Y X

Line of the scissors or straddle approach

3-strides radius

Alternative lines of approach of the Fosbury Flop

① ② ③

Fig 1 Before attempting the high jump it is necessary to establish a safe and accurately fixed take-off

The take-off surface needs to be reasonably flat and firm. Synthetic surfaces are unsafe in wet weather, particularly for inexperienced jumpers who are not wearing special footwear with heel spikes.

The bar

Since 'floppers' and straddle jumpers land on their backs, they are in danger of landing on the bar and thereby injuring themselves should they knock it off. It is for this reason that round bars are now mandatory. However, these are still painful to land on, and thus the use of elastic bars for training has become common practice. The elastic bar exerts inward pressure, so it is a sensible precaution either to place heavy weights on the upright footings, or to push them under the bed itself. This prevents the stands from being pulled inwards on to athletes who may land on the bar.

Equipment

The training facility must be able to provide a safe landing area with a flat, firm approach and at least two uprights (or stands) on which to support the crossbar. Several bars are needed since they do get broken from time to time.

You can get by as a high jumper without any special equipment of your own at all. Vests, shorts and running shoes will suffice for competition, while warm overclothing such as a track suit is all that is needed in addition for warm-up or training. Shoes which have screw-in spikes are best, since they can be easily changed to accommodate different types of runway surfaces. Most modern shoes are made this way. Better, and safer still are the special high jump shoes which have heel spikes in order to secure the take-off foot when it is planted. These shoes may also be stiffened to give lateral support, and thickened slightly at the sole to assist the take-off. Some brands are so sophisticated that they are specifically designed either for flop jumping, or straddle jumping. Such shoes are very expensive, but fortunately you only need one for the take-off foot – a normal running shoe will do for the other.

The high jumper may additionally need a 30 m measuring tape with which to measure out his approach run (see page 9), and marking tape, or powder such as talcum powder or scouring powder, with which to mark key parts of it.

The jump

The scissors style of jump provides the basis for jumping high because it, more than any other style of high jumping, channels the jumper's energy in a vertical direction. Because it develops good take-off technique it provides the core training component for all of the world's top jumpers. It is the best form of jump for beginners to learn, as well as being the only safe means of jumping into sand pits.

Having said that, it is important to distinguish between the straight leg scissors jump and the bent leg variety. The latter is more important in relation to the flop since the more natural straight leg version has the lead leg pivoting like a long lever around the hip and is totally

1 The bent leg scissor jump

inappropriate. It is useful when executing this jump to imagine that the movement is being carried out within the confines of a large glass tube which you must not break.

Approach run

All high jump approach runs need to be shorter than those of the other jumping events. This is because a fast approach doesn't allow high jumpers sufficient time in which to create vertical force as they pass over their take-off foot. However, the curved flop approach can be longer and quicker than those of its counterparts.

The approach run for the scissors jump should be straight (set at an angle of about 30° to the plane of the crossbar) as with the approaches for straddle jump and the western roll. The scissors approach run will usually be between five and eight strides long, depending upon which run configuration is preferred (odd or even).

The most common form of flop approach has the shape of an inverted walking stick (number 2 in figure 1). The fully curved approach (number 1), at one time popular for introducing first principles, is now seldom seen. The third variety, set at a more obtuse angle, reduces the risk of slipping in wet weather. However, it also reduces the natural rotation of the jumper's body around its long axis after take-off (necessary for turning his back towards the bar) and affects the essence of the jump. In addition, this third option tends to make the jumper travel along the bar, thereby increasing the likelihood of dislodging it and also landing off the bed. Final choice of approach is a highly individual matter, and the product of much trial and error.

The simplest method of establishing individual flop approaches for large groups of beginners is for the teacher/coach to pace out two modified zig-zags, 3 strides × 3 strides × 3 strides, commencing just in front of the base of each upright (figure 2). This will produce an eight-stride approach for most youngsters, provided that they toe the start mark with their take-off foot.

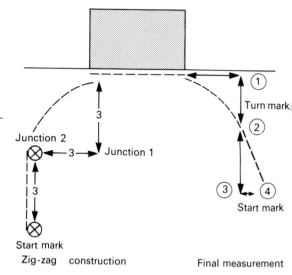

Fig 2 **Establishing, then measuring 'flop' approach runs**

Those taking off from their right foot approach from the left side of the landing area, while those taking off from their left foot approach from the right. This principle also holds true for the scissors jumper. Both styles of jumping thus involve taking off from the foot which is furthest away from the upright. Straddle jumpers approach from the same side as their take-off foot, and jump from the foot which is closer to the upright. Markers placed at the second junction and at the farthest point provide guidance for the start and the turn.

The group can finely tune their own starting positions by slightly shortening or lengthening the run in relation to the teacher/coach's mark, depending upon whether or not they are consistently beyond or behind the correct take-off position. Those who are beyond it will need to lengthen their run behind the start-mark, while those who arrive short of the take-off point will need to shorten their run by that amount.

The final four strides of the approach run should follow a curve. If they do not begin at a point corresponding to the turn-mark, which has been roughly established in pacing out the initial pattern, then the mark must eventually be moved to the point at which the jumper's foot made contact with the ground, four strides out from the take-off.

Approaches suitable for individual athletes can be constructed by starting at the take-off point and running back around the curve for the desired number of strides. Having marked that spot a few test runs, with adjustments if necessary, will soon establish a reliable pattern. Coaches to top-class athletes are very particular about the accurate measurement of the curve run by their jumpers over these final strides. However, the criteria by which they assess and judge this varies almost as much as the numbers of coaches involved at this level.

For the Fosbury approach the jumper first measures from the base of the nearer upright, as if an extension of the crossbar, until he is at right angles to the turn-mark (number 1 in figure 2). From there he measures out to that mark (2) and again from it (3), until he is at right angles to the start-mark, up to which he takes the final measurement (4). The jumper must then remember or record these four distances. The measurement for a straight-line approach involves two distances or the first three measurements.

Preparation for take-off

Once the jumper has begun to 'run the turn' he will tend to lean towards the centre of the curve in order to stay balanced. The modern trend is for the best jumpers to exaggerate this tendency and actually lean slightly inwards. These final strides need to be shortened and quickened, as foot contact with the ground shifts from the ball of the foot (as in the normal running action) to the heel of the take-off foot which makes the initial contact. This is followed by a roll from the heel across the sole of the take-off foot, finishing high on the toes just before contact with the ground is broken.

During these final few strides the arms no longer synchronise with the legs but are withdrawn behind the hips, while the hips themselves are lowered in order to prepare the jumping leg. In jumps which have very slow approach speeds the latter may be a conscious act, but in the Fosbury flop where relatively fast approach runs are employed, this must not

be so. Indeed, the focal point of the coaching ought to be exactly the opposite, that is to keep the hips high and to think of the movement as 'running off the ground'.

The withdrawal of the arms usually commences with a slight forwards movement, while the elbows are lifted away from the body in a movement which circles forwards and outwards. The circling of the elbows continues until they come back close to and behind the body.

Take-off

The actual point of take-off needs to be close to the nearer upright both for safety (see page 10), and so that it is far enough out from the plane of the bar to ensure that the highest point of the flight path followed by the jumper's centre of gravity occurs directly over the bar. If the high point occurs in front of the bar, the start of the approach should be moved closer. If it occurs beyond the bar, the start should be moved further away. The ideal spot for the take-off is thus some 70 cm out from the base of the nearer upright, and 70 cm in towards the opposite upright (see figure 1).

The take-off foot should be planted in line with the final line of the approach run (that is at a tangent to the curve around which the athlete has run). It should never be turned in towards the centre of the curve, that is away from the landing area – to do so is to commit a grave error.

As the take-off foot contacts the ground, the hips should be squeezed forwards and upwards. This action should trigger a similar, simultaneous arm drive, accompanied by vigorous use of the free leg as weight is transferred forwards and the point of contact with the ground passes from heel to toe. In the standard scissors jump the free leg is kept straight and swung from the hip. In the flop style, and its modified scissors precursor, the leg remains bent as the thigh is thrust forwards and upwards. This is mainly because the curved final approach makes it extremely difficult to swing a straight leg. Since the advent of the flop style of jumping top-class high jumpers have at various intervals attempted to incorporate a straighter free leg into their technique, but no one has yet been successful enough to establish it as the norm.

All take-off energies should be channelled vertically and so it is helpful if the high jumper thinks of directing them up through the top of the head, slightly away from the landing area, or towards the centre of the curve around which he is running. The jumper thus avoids the second sin of take-off; that of anticipating rotation over the bar, channelling energy in the direction of the bed and losing lift in the process. Keeping the shoulder nearer the bar as high as possible, or raising that arm through take-off, also helps to avoid this error.

The jumper should end the take-off and leave the ground with full extension. The chest should be high, the torso upright with the pelvis placed directly beneath it, and all the joints in the take-off leg fully stretched.

2 Take-off for the Fosbury Flop

3 The hips are kept high and the jumper runs off the ground

4 The jumper drives vertically to clear the bar

5 and 6
For this stage of the jump
it is important to relax
and to keep the hips high

7 The landing for the
Fosbury flop

Off the ground

Once off the ground there is nothing that jumpers can do to change the path of their centre of gravity. They should instead lie back and enjoy it!

They can, however, change the displacement of the body around its centre of gravity, and this is very significant. As a general rule, moving the extremities of curved body shapes towards each other maintains the shape of the curve and prevents the mid-section from sagging (see photograph 8). Thus floppers can prevent the hips from dropping and dislodging the bar as long as they maintain the body curve by squeezing the feet towards the head, and the head towards the feet.

As they rotate around the bar, floppers subconsciously anticipate landing and tuck the chin on to the chest. This has the effect of straightening the lower legs, finally enabling the heels to clear the bar. To a large extent nature again takes care of itself, although this quite instinctive response will create difficulties if the bar is low or if the landing bed is deep. Floppers should, therefore, pull the heels in and maintain the back-arch for as long as they dare. It is possible to assist final bar clearance by

8 It is important to maintain the back (or body) arch when executing the flop

straightening the legs as they are pulled towards the head, or by folding the thighs in towards the chest. Correct timing of these actions is essential for successful execution.

Landing

In a correctly executed flop the jumper will land on his back, high up on his shoulders. The alignment of the body as it makes contact with the bed will indicate whether or not the preceding elements have been correctly accomplished. Floppers should generally land aligned at right angles to the bar.

Because scissors jumpers land on one foot (the free, or non-take-off one), foam landing areas are not very safe and great care must be taken, particularly when the foam is soft and there is danger of the jumper landing either between modules or on the edge of the bed.

Aids to training

Jumping to raise the hips to a pre-set target, such as a high bar or a handkerchief tied high on an upright provides a useful means of focusing attention on vertical lift. An alternative way of doing this is to stack three individual modules one upon the other and jump aiming to get the shoulders on to the top (see photograph 9).

Scissors jumpers will benefit from jumping to touch a high target with their free leg. This is not such a useful practice for flop jumpers since the leg-swing is of an entirely different nature from that used in the jump proper.

Beat boards, Reuter boards, and take-off boxes are useful in creating the feeling of lift at take-off, as well as affording the jumper more time in the air to work on flight techniques. Floppers can gain flight awareness by doing two-footed jumps from high boxes or benches (photograph 10). Useful work can also be done from trampettes, provided that you are extra careful about how the take-off foot is placed on the webbing; the jumper can be thrown unexpectedly sideways if it is not placed 'dead centre'.

9 A high jump practice on to modules to encourage the jumper to go high

10 Flop lay-out practice from a high box

Learning

1.   Experiment to find the preferred take-off foot.

2.   Mark a circle of 50 cm radius by the base of the upright opposite the side of the bed to the take-off foot.

3.   Pace out the rough zig-zag guide as described earlier in this chapter.

4.   Practise the approach run from the start-mark, toeing it with the take-off foot. The run ought to be approximately eight strides long. Make minor adjustments until it is accurate and reliable.

5.   At the end of the run either do a high hop to land on your take-off leg without landing on the bed, or do a bent leg scissors jump on to it. Set a low bar and gradually raise it as your confidence improves.

6.   Practise the 'lay-out' by standing close to the bed with your back to it. Do a two-footed jump backwards on to the bed in the manner of a trampoline 'back-drop'. Once competent, introduce a bar and gradually raise it as you improve.

7.   Return to your curved approach run. Run it and take off to clear the bar and land on your shoulders in the correct manner. Raise the bar as you gain in confidence.

LONG JUMP

Long jumpers have to be both fast and springy. Top-class long jumpers tend to be tall and long-legged.

Safety

Although the event is not inherently dangerous, injury can be caused by competing and training on runways which are pitted by the footmarks of previous users, and by pits which are undug, inadequately dug, or which conceal buried debris. A little time spent before use, raking cinder runways and properly preparing pits, is invaluable.

Badly worn take-off boards, and those which protrude above the level of the runway, are a different matter. They are a serious and frequent source of injury. However, responsibility for correcting such faults rests with the owners of the facility and their ground staff rather than with jumper and coach. Avoid bad boards like the plague, and report the faults to those responsible for correcting them; they are legally obliged to ensure that they are safe.

Equipment

Long jumpers do not require as much specialised personal equipment as their high jumping counterparts. However, it is useful to have screw-in spikes which fit into a ribbed sole, so that you have maximum grip on the board in wet weather. Although 5 mm or 6 mm spikes will be adequate on a modern synthetic surface in dry conditions, longer spikes of 9 mm may be necessary in the wet. You may find that you require 12 mm or 15 mm spikes on cinder or grass runways, even when it is not raining.

If foot lengths are not used, a 30 m tape measure may be necessary in order to measure out the approach run, and markers will be necessary if accuracy, or 'cue', check-marks, are used. Training shoes will often suffice for this purpose. Remember that the rules do not permit these check-marks to be placed on the runway itself.

Approach run

Because their event enables them to run nearer to maximum speed than jumpers in other disciplines, long jumpers tend to have the longest approach runs. General guidelines covering the establishment of appropriate approaches have already been outlined on page 9. The final form chosen must be capable of bringing the jumper accurately and regularly on to the take-off board at his optimum take-off speed.

There are three methods of starting an approach run for long jump. The first, which now finds less favour than it used to, involves the jumper standing at the mark with both feet together, making the first stride with the take-off leg. This produces a run composed of an odd number of running strides. A currently popular method is to commence the run from a position in which the athlete toes the start-mark with one foot forward. Since it is a very rare occurrence for jumpers to then use the same foot for their first stride, toeing the mark with the take-off foot will produce a run of an even configuration. Use of the non-take-off foot will have the opposite effect. More experienced jumpers often walk or jog on to their start-mark, placing one foot opposite it as they do so. The foot which is chosen will determine the subsequent configuration of the run.

Novices tend to be most inconsistent in the execution of the approach, particularly in the first stride. Therefore a check-mark placed at this spot will be of great help to them throughout the early learning period, and it can be easily discarded when they improve.

Accuracy check marks must be placed far enough away from the take-off board to permit the jumper to stop before crossing its front edge, otherwise officials will credit the run as an attempted jump. A 'cue' mark, signifying a change in emphasis to staccato running, is often useful over the final few strides. For training purposes, special short runs about eight strides long reduce stress on the athlete, and permit the take-off action to be practised at a slower speed.

The full approach run should be composed of three parts: a beginning, which may be either a gradual build up of speed or a more rapid acceleration; a middle phase which will be faster if the beginning is slow, and a conservation of speed if it has been fast; and a final stage in which emphasis is placed upon increasing leg speed over the last few strides. The middle phase should be used by the athlete to align the body in an upright position, ready for take-off. The phases are often referred to as Acceleration/Alignment/Attack and they would occupy six strides each in an eighteen-stride approach.

Preparation for take-off

This takes place very early in the approach run. Coaches are becoming more and more aware that athletes make judgements as to whether or not they will strike the board correctly quite early in the run. Many make automatic adjustments in order to bring this about, others make the wrong adjustments or the wrong judgements, and fail badly as a result. Thus it is helpful for athletes to be aware that they will need to make such decisions, and to do so as early as possible, in order to eradicate the risk of fouls.

Bringing the trunk into an erect position during the middle phase of the run begins the preparation proper. (This is necessary because the jumper will have to concentrate on other things during the attack phase.) While this is happening the hips must be brought forwards directly under the torso just as in the high jump.

Although the hips will sink slightly during the final few strides into the take-off this must not be sought deliberately on any account. The jumper must instead concentrate on maintaining height through this phase.

Take-off

The final stride should be shorter and quicker than those leading up to it. The hips must stay forwards under the trunk, which remains erect, with the chest leading.

A quick placement of the take-off foot precipitates the vigorous free leg action which is so characteristic of the long jumper at take-off (photographs 11–13). First of all the leg is folded (the tighter the better) and then pulled past the supporting leg, before being thrust forwards and upwards to finish with the thigh level with the hip. Pointing the toe towards the pit spoils this position while pulling it up towards the knee enhances it.

When the jumper breaks contact with the take-off board there should be maximum extension of all the joint complexes in the take-off leg (see photograph 13). Maintaining an active sprinting arm action into, and right through, take-off will also contribute to lift. Both arms punch high in the take-off action (one forwards and the other backwards).

Cues such as 'drive up through the hips' – 'feel the skin tighten behind your take-off knee' – 'feel the stretch at the ankle joint' or 'punch the free leg, or the arms skywards' can all help to give the jumper a good focus for what he is attempting to do.

Since take-off constitutes such a vital part of the jump, it requires much drilling in order to get it right. This is best done from a special, short approach run of about eight strides long.

11 Take-off for the stride-style long jump

12 The free leg is punched upwards

13, 14 and 15 (top, facing page) **For the flight stage the body is upright and the thighs are kept apart**

15

16 The athlete's feet reach outwards

17 The long jumper rocks forwards on landing

Off the ground

All movements in the air should contribute towards maintaining balance and checking unhelpful forward rotation, which is the natural by-product of the take-off. Long, extended body shapes are more useful in this respect than tucked ones. It was for this reason that the 'sail' style of jumping so readily adopted by novices, was superseded by forms such as the 'hang' and the 'hitch-kick'. However, many modern jumpers have discarded these styles too, particularly the hitch-kick, because either they are not really effective or they are too complicated. Instead jumpers are holding on to their take-off position and maintaining a vertical trunk, before bringing their take-off leg forward at the very last minute in order to effect their landing. This technique is referred to as the 'stride' jump. The arms follow a natural, circling sequence of movement in flight, assisting the jumper's balance in the process.

Landing

Once the legs are both out in front of the body, forward rotation will resume, and the feet will drop prematurely to the pit. This is why the final action must be delayed.

Jumpers must try to keep their heels high until they cut the sand. At this stage it is more helpful for the hands to be behind the body rather than in front, because they can then be thrown forwards on impact to help prevent the athlete sitting back and losing distance.

Dropping one foot before the other is a bad habit which can bring about unnecessary defeat in close contests. Success or failure in controlling this will be evident in the sand when you have completed the jump.

Aids to training

The way in which the take-off leads to height and flight in the jump is one of the most difficult things for the inexperienced long jumper to become aware of. A light object suspended above head height, or a target such as a handkerchief tied to a post or javelin may be provided as a focus for the jumper. Since the jumper's centre of gravity is positioned somewhere within the pelvis, then raising the hips to a target creates an appropriate objective.

Gymnastic beat boards or springboards can be usefully employed to aid the take-off so that the jumper gets a feeling of height and flight. Similarly, a home-made box (photograph 18) or three or four gymnastic benches laid side by side may be used, provided that one is especially careful to ensure that the benches are constantly kept close together.

Corrections to a lazy 'leg-shoot' on landing can be made effectively by heaping up a pile of sand just before the point of landing, or by placing a soft marker in the pit (photograph 19). In both instances the aim should be to land beyond the marker.

Because they find it difficult to be accurate while concentrating upon other things, young novice jumpers will derive great benefit from making the jump from a special, metre square, take-off board rather than the regulation 122 cm × 20 cm one.

Learning

1. Experiment to find the preferred take-off foot.
2. Stand facing away from the pit, toeing the edge of the board nearer the pit where it joins the no-jump indicator (the centre of the board if a special one is being used), then pace out six or eight 'giant' strides and place a marker.
3. Practise a strong but relaxed approach run from the start-mark, toeing the mark with the take-off foot. The run should be six or eight strides long, depending upon how many giant strides were taken at the outset. Make minor adjustments until the approach is accurate and reliable.
4. Run and jump, holding the take-off position and landing on your take-off leg. The jump should be high, but not long.
5. Repeat point 4 but take a giant step with the free leg after the take-off leg has landed in the sand.

18 A good long jump practice involves using a take-off box for height and a hip-high target upon which to focus

6. Repeat point 5 but try to hold the sole of the free leg so that it can be seen clearly by someone standing at the far end of the pit.
7. Finally, run, jump and hold the free leg position in flight, before landing on both feet. Work hard to delay the take-off leg coming through to land. This action should involve folding the leg forwards then stretching it outwards. It is essentially a bent leg action.

19 Improving landing technique

TRIPLE JUMP

Triple jumpers have similar physiques and abilities to long jumpers. However, because of the quite stressful nature of the event, approach runs are seldom as fast or as long as in long jump, so slower athletes possessing other qualities can still do well. The event also demands and develops qualities of physical resilience.

Since 1988 triple jump has been accepted by the International Amateur Athletics Federation (IAAF) as an official event for women, and national associations are encouraged to develop their participation.

Safety

The triple jumper needs to take the same care as the long jumper to ensure that the pit, the take-off board and the runway are safe. However, the triple jumper must pay particular attention to the runway between the pit and the board because it is on here that the two single-footed landings will have to be made under some stress.

When injury does occur, as it inevitably will, you should rest immediately, seek knowledgeable medical help, and follow that advice until the injury has healed. This may involve complete rest or just abstinence from jumping, depending upon the severity of the injury. When the condition has cleared up then training can be resumed gradually.

Equipment

Great care must be taken in the selection of footwear. Specialist triple jump shoes should be strengthened and have flat heel sections. Where you have to make do with sprinting spikes, try to avoid those with fabric sides or those which have a curved section on the base of the heel. Additional heel padding is advisable. A thin, tailored piece of sponge rubber inserted into the heel of each shoe will help, or you could try the special plastic 'heel cups' which are available through specialist outlets. To get hold of the latter you should make enquiries of your national association.

Like his long jumping counterpart, the triple jumper will possibly need a 30 m measuring tape and some means of marking check-marks.

Approach run

Other than being a shade slower, the triple jump approach is almost identical with that of long jump. The speed of the run will be determined largely by the jumper's ability to control the hop and step landings at speed. The optimum speed is thus the product of trial and error over many training sessions. Novices frequently make the error of approaching faster than they can handle.

Preparation for take-off

At the beginning this will not differ much from that of long jump. As ability improves, changes will have to take place which bring the jumper's hips and trunk further forward over the take-off foot so that the take-off is directed more forwards than upwards.

Take-off

The jump should be organised so that the first (hop) take-off is from the stronger leg, that is if the jumper has a preference. Doing so ensures that two out of the three take-offs are made from this leg.

It has already been suggested that the triple jumper should come on to the board and leave it with the body slightly further forward than the long jumper. This is because the three phases of the jump, each with its own retardation on landing, will progressively result in substantial loss of horizontal momentum, making it doubly important for the jumper to maximise horizontal force at the outset.

Quality triple jumpers, like high jumpers, employ simultaneous, forward arm actions at take-off in order to maximise total force output. However, the modern trend is away from doing this on the hop take-off, since the outcome will be to retard speed both in the first take-off and thus through the remainder of the jump.

20 and 21 (top and below left) **For the triple jump the athlete runs 'off' the board**

22 The hop section must be low and controlled

23 The landing leg should remain active

24, 25 and 26 (above right, below left and right) **The free leg is kept hip high for as long as possible during the step phase of the jump**

27 and 28 (right) **The athlete goes for height on the final take-off**

29 The landing is the same as for long jump

Off the ground

The hop

The flight path of the hop should not be too high if you are to conserve horizontal momentum, and lessen the shock of landing. The jumper must keep the trunk erect (head up and chest out) and at the same time maintain general balance. The position of the arms helps with this, but just before landing they must be drawn behind the body in order to prepare for their simultaneous use through the step take-off. Think of moving the elbows back rather than swinging straight arms (see high jump).

Just before regaining contact with the ground at the end of this phase of the jump, the take-off leg is brought in front of the body. The leg should then reach out and back as contact is made, so that the sole of the foot strikes the ground moving backwards in a clawing action. A secondary effect of this action will be a backward displacement of the free leg, which is important for the step take-off.

At the moment of landing the arms are swung forwards ahead of the body in order to assist the movement.

The step

This is the most critical part of the jump. Novices are generally unable to give it as much emphasis as it requires, either because they have insufficient specific triple jump strength or, more often than not, because they precede the step by too big and high a hop. The net result is that the phase finishes up far too short. Less distance in the hop (the result of better control of direction), and greater effort in the step provide a sure remedy.

Very active use of the thigh of the free leg will help to channel force into this take-off, particularly if emphasis is placed on the pulling action from behind the body. This takes place in concert with the double arm action.

That done, good triple jumpers then become kamikaze experts. The longer they can hold on to flight, repeating the erect, head-up characteristics of the hop phase, and delay setting down their 'landing gear', the further they will travel.

During flight good jumpers squeeze the foreleg back under the thigh in preparation for the landing. Once again the landing action should be an active 'out-and-back' clawing one. The arms, which have been withdrawn behind the body, are swung forwards simultaneously to assist the final take-off.

The jump

Diminishing forward speed, coupled with the fact that the take-off must now be from the weaker leg, means that there is little flight time available for a sophisticated jump technique. Most triple jumpers adopt a 'sail' style for this phase and concentrate on going for height. Some jumpers modify their landing by sliding sideways rather than rocking forwards over their feet.

Balance between effort and distance

Because the hop is often overdone and the step underdone, guidance is often needed concerning how to balance the two phases. To bring about the best overall outcome, novices should use a ratio of 10:8:9. A 10 ft hop, followed by a 8 ft step and completed by a 9 ft jump will thus produce a jump totalling 27 ft. Similarly a 15 ft hop, 12 ft step, and 13 ft 6 in jump (same ratio) would produce one of 40 ft 6 in. Working metrically all through one would have to produce individual elements of 4.07 m:3.26 m and 3.67 m for an 11 m effort. High-calibre jumpers who are also good technicians have a more even balance between phases.

Effort distribution is quite a different matter. Because momentum is high at the outset and low at the end, the amount of effort which the jumper needs to put into each individual phase must increase as the jump progresses.

Aids to training

Jumping and bounding routines of the types discussed on pages 85 and 86 are the stock in trade of the triple jumper. Much training time is normally devoted to these routines in order to improve the jumper's strength for the event. By practising them the jumper will also train his 'feel' for the rhythm of the event.

My personal inclination is away from this type of training. The triple jump event is so stressful to the lower limbs and the spine that most adult triple jumpers spend more time injured than competing. Why seek such an outcome by selecting training regimes which heighten the effect? Why not seek to develop strength by methods which place less stress on leg structures?

One way of maintaining the correct balance between jump phases during practice is to jump to markers placed at specified distances. These can be teased out a little at a time in order to act as focus for effort on the way to improvement. It must not be forgotten, however, that working off short approach runs makes it necessary to modify the positions of these markers.

Learning

1. Experiment to find out which is the preferred take-off foot.
2. Measure some standing long jumps made from a single-footed take-off (from one foot to both feet), alternating the take-off foot in order to find out which is the stronger. If this indicates that the stronger foot is not the naturally preferred one, some awkward decisions have to be made.
3. Stand with the chosen foot forward and hop to land on it. Follow this by stepping on to your other foot, and finally jump on to both feet. Say to yourself 'same foot – other foot – both feet' as you do it.
4. Repeat point 3 from the position in which you start toeing the start line or mark.
5. Build a rhythm into the entire jump.
6. Walk to the start line and repeat the jump.
7. Build up the speed of approach by developing the walk into a jog or a run. At this stage an individual can use markers profitably to control phase distances, or a group or class can

work on a triple jump 'grid' (figure 3). The objective when working on such a grid must be for each individual to try to progress as far as possible towards the side where the spacings are greatest, while still being able to land *on* each line. This enables all jumpers to work at their own optimum level.

All landings should, in essence, be flat-footed, and during all take-offs the free thigh should be pulled through from behind the supporting leg to hip height.

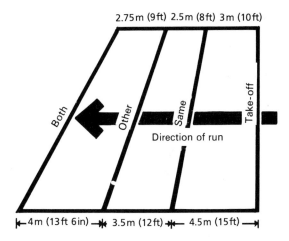

Fig 3 **The triple jump training grid**

POLE VAULT

Pole vaulters are the tumblers in the athletics 'circus'. They need to possess good gymnastic ability above all other qualities. The ability to run quickly is an added asset which makes it possible for the vaulter to hold the pole higher and to use stiffer poles which recoil with more force, thus projecting him to greater heights.

Although height can be an advantage in helping to use and bend stiffer poles (and contemporary top-class vaulters do tend to reflect such a trend), gymnastic ability, which seems more common in those of smaller stature, is such an overriding factor that tall vaulters are still the exception rather than the rule.

Safety

The pole vault is without doubt the event possessing the greatest potential for personal danger in field athletics. Fortunately, the dangers are so obvious that injuries do not feature that strongly in practice. Great care must be taken to ensure that all equipment is well maintained, for it is in its malfunctioning that greatest danger lies.

Landing areas must be at least 5 m square. Foam areas or beds are a must when using modern fibre glass poles, and for these the minimum specification excludes the two protective pads which extend either side of the box into which the pole is planted. These pads provide additional protection in case the pole, with the vaulter on it, fails to reach the vertical.

As in high jump, it is essential that the individual units of the landing area are securely fastened together and are covered by a continuous cover sheet, in order to prevent the athlete accidentally slipping between them.

If sand is the only form of landing area available then the only safe pole to use is an old-fashioned metal or wooden one. Because they don't bend, these poles enable vaulters to land on their feet. Building the sand up a metre high is recommended if vaulting is taking place higher than 3 metres.

Fibre glass poles are fragile and will snap if misused. Care must be taken to avoid:

- bending the pole beyond 90°
- bending the pole against its natural, built-in bend (photograph 30)
- using it in a planting box which has its back set at right angles to its base (modern boxes for fibre glass vaulting have this set at an angle of 105° to the base)
- getting it scratched (keep it safely in its delivery carton when not actually in use)
- using the pole with a damaged end-bung.

The use of elastic crossbars for training purposes prevents injury resulting from landing on the bar, or being hit by it after it has been dislodged. They also dispense with the tedious chore of having to wind the stands down and replace the bar each time that it is hit.

Equipment

The vaulter wears much the same clothing as the long jumper. However, special shoes other than sprinting spikes are not needed.

On the other hand, the fibre glass pole is the most specialised piece of personal equipment in field athletics. The choice is quite wide and several makes and types of pole are available. The thin-walled varieties such as the American Catapole, Pacer, Skypole, and Spirit poles, are light to carry and are the competition

30 The pole will settle with its soft side underneath

pace-setters. A thick-walled, durable, but heavy pole is also produced by Bantex. Careful selection of the right pole to suit the vaulter's needs is critical both to performance and safety. Each manufacturer produces a wide range of models of each type of pole. These differ in length and resistance to bending or stiffness.

The vaulter selects according to his body-weight and the height at which he wishes to hold the pole (a tolerance of some 12 in is possible). Thus someone weighing 140 lb seeking a grip at about 11 ft 6 in to 12 ft 6 in will select a 13 ft long pole. Such a pole will have a model number approximating to 13040 (13 referring to the 13 ft total length, and 040 to the 140 lb weight), the actual arrangement of figures reflecting the particular whim of the maker. Metric model classification is slowly gaining ground.

As if this were not complex enough, poles of each model number differ from each other, some being slightly stiffer than others. To cater for this, each is assigned a flex number additional to the model number, and this is usually written in indelible ink at the grip end of the pole. Such information is really only important to the very best vaulters. It is of little value to the novice.

Vaulters are permitted by the rules to tape their poles in order to improve grip, but this is limited to no more than two layers thick. Linen adhesive tape is best for this purpose, and can be specially purchased from pole suppliers. Start at the position of the bottom hand and wrap the tape spirally, working up the pole until the full length of the hand hold is covered. It is also sensible to tape the base of the pole in order to protect it from chafing against the back of the box.

A substance called Venice turpentine, smeared on the hands, is useful for making the grip even more secure. It can be easily made by dissolving powdered resin in pure turpentine – not to be confused with turpentine substitute which is easier to obtain. Modern adhesive sprays such as 'Photo-mount' offer a most effective alternative.

30 m measuring tapes, markers for check-marks, spare bungs, spare adhesive tape and a towel with which to dry the pole in wet conditions, are also useful pieces of equipment.

Approach run

Before starting, you need to ascertain which is the 'soft side' of the pole, and then mark it so that it can be correctly held and carried without overstressing it. This can be done by supporting

31 The 'soft side' of this pole is clearly marked

one or both ends of the pole off the ground, and then letting it roll so that it settles in its most natural position (photograph 30). The pole will lie in such a way that it sags towards the ground. The lower (ground) side of that sag represents the 'soft side' of the pole. This should be marked with a piece of adhesive tape if it hasn't already been indicated by the pole manufacturer. The 'soft side' should be facing the sky as the vaulter stands at the start of his run.

The basic principles of the pole vault approach are identical to those of the horizontal jumps, except that the vaulter must carry his pole, which modifies the nature and speed of the run. Short, eight-stride approaches are very appropriate for beginners using soft poles.

Most pole vaulters are right-handed and the following instructions are directed at them. Left-handed readers will need to transpose the underlined instructions.

Toe the start mark with your left foot, holding the nearer end of the pole which is at the shoulder, in your right hand, and using an undergrasp. Grasp the pole with the left hand in front of the chest in an overgrasp, so that your hands are about 60 cm apart. As the weight is rocked back on the rear foot just before commencing the run, shift the hands to hip level on the right. In so doing you will turn the right hand so that its palm faces outwards, with the thumb to the rear, and place downward pressure on the pole to raise its opposite tip off the ground.

Learn to run quickly while keeping the pole steady and holding its tip just above eye level. There is a tendency to point the pole slightly to the left. During the first part of the full approach, concentrate on building up speed. Change to fast leg speed during the final strides into the take-off, in the same way that other jumpers do.

Preparation for take-off

In pole vault this phase is called 'the plant'. The 'plant' begins during the third stride before take-off, as the left foot moves forward. The pole is lowered and pushed towards the planting box. This continues as the right foot is grounded, and progresses in a forwards and upwards manner into the following stride. By the time that the take-off foot has been finally grounded the distant end of the pole will have contacted the back of the box, and will be beginning to bend forwards, upwards and outwards as pressure is directed down it. The vaulter's arms should be extended overhead, with the left elbow tucked in under the pole.

At this stage, if using a metal or a wooden pole, it is normal for the pole to be pushed through the bottom hand as the plant is made. However, this should not happen in fibre glass vaulting, and since all metal pole vaulters will eventually have to transfer on to fibre glass poles if they show any ability, it can be argued that this aspect of metal vaulting should be deliberately ignored.

Inexperienced vaulters tend to delay the plant. This will prevent them from attaining the extended arm position at take-off, producing a rushed, unbalanced result and a landing on the bed off to the jumper's right. Therefore, like the good gardener, plant early for the best results.

Take-off

The right-handed vaulter will take off from his left foot, which should be placed directly underneath the right hand upon the completion of the plant. It is equally important that the take-off foot is underneath the pole, neither offset to any side nor pointing sideways, because otherwise faults will become manifest later on in the vault.

The actual take-off action is not unlike that of the long jumper. It is a forward and upward jump from the ground, showing a high, free thigh and good extension of the supporting leg, with perhaps more emphasis placed on forward rather than upward drive. This helps the athlete to channel more energy into the pole. Body and hip placement, similar to that of the long jumper at take-off, also assists the pole vaulter.

It is important that the arms are kept fixed in their take-off position in order to keep the vaulter from closing the chest to the pole, which is a bad fault. Space between vaulter and pole must be maintained. Pressing down the pole with the top hand adds to the forces which make the pole bend.

Off the ground

Once off the ground the vaulter should 'hang' momentarily in the take-off position (that is with the take-off leg extended and the free leg bent), in order to increase the bend in the pole. This delay is quite slight, for the vaulter must get the hips above the head before the pole unbends.

The tuck (or rock-back) which makes this possible to achieve, must be both rapid and tight.

32 and 33 (above and below left) **The plant is early and high for the pole vault**

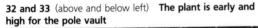

34 The take-off is under the top hand

33

35 and 36 (below) **It is important to stay away from the pole during the hang and rock-back stages**

37 and 38 (below, left)
The pull–push phase

39 Bar clearance for the pole vault

40 Running over low obstacles helps to develop a well balanced run

The head is thrown backwards as the hips are rolled up and above the shoulders, aided by a strong swing of the take-off leg. The top arm must remain relatively long so that the rock-back occurs around the fulcrum of the shoulders.

The timing of the rock-back is critical: too soon and the pole will be prevented from reaching the vertical; too late and the vaulter will fail to get his hips into position for vertical projection when they leave the pole.

Once inverted, the vaulter should bring the body close to the pole in order to facilitate the handstand on the pole which occurs towards the end of the 'pull–push' phase. This phase commences as a pull of the left hand, quickly followed by a push by the right. The vaulter ought then to be able to look down his pole into the box.

Vaulters using fibre glass poles leave them

41–5 Backward roll into a handstand. This improves ability at the top of the vault

with a rotation which takes them on to their backs. To some extent this will take care of bar clearance. Turning the thumbs inwards will help the arms to clear.

Landing

Much of the mechanics of landing for the fibre glass vaulter is explained in the previous paragraph. Vaulters landing from metal or wooden poles will tend to land on their feet. Any extraneous movements will tend to disturb natural processes and create problems therefore they should avoid making them.

Aids to training

Running with the pole is a special skill which should be practised, for example, with high knee raises, carrying the pole. Weight should be on the balls of the feet, and the hips should be carried slightly forwards – that is the running should be well balanced. The drill can also be done over low obstacles such as canes (photograph 40) or low hurdles.

Floor exercises of a gymnastic type, such as hand-balancing, cart-wheels, arab springs, donkey jumps and backward roll to handstand (photographs 41–5) are good for building shoulder strength and developing skills useful to the pull–push phase of the vault.

Swinging activities such as skinning the cat, heave vaults, muscle-ups, up-starts, upward and downward circles, and grand circles on ropes, vertical and horizontal bars and beams, again contribute to shoulder strength and develop the skills of the post take-off hang and rock-back. The rock-back can be improved by doing 'pop-ups' using the pole (photograph 46). These are performed from a short approach, and the vaulter remains close to the pole in the inverted position until both pole and athlete come down on the bed.

Take-off drills (photographs 47–9) are helpful

43

44

45

46 The 'pop up'

to beginners provided that they are discouraged from getting close to the pole and rotating around it. It is not a good idea for beginners to learn and practise the rotation which brings them belly down over the bar, and back towards the bed. Natural processes bring this movement about because 'locked in' forces are released when the pole straightens. Instead, the beginner should keep the hips and the shoulder facing forwards for as long as possible, while vaulting as high as possible. In this way the forces that are stored in the pole at take-off will be maximised rather than diminished through premature anticipation of the clearance movement.

Technique for coming off the top of the pole can be improved by practising at heights which commence 30 cm below the vaulter's best before quickly progressing to 10 to 15 cm above it, irrespective of success. This helps the vaulter to learn to 'live' at that height. Similar work can be done by placing the bar way beyond the vaulter's best mark, with uprights set well

towards him (see Rules section p. 92) so that he can work to get the soles of his feet against the bar.

It is relatively easy to run very fast and hold high. This enables reasonable heights to be cleared. However, the true essence of vaulting rests in the height that the vaulter can clear above his top hand, and this is the goal towards which training effort should be channelled.

Learning

Remember that right-handed vaulters must take off from their left foot. Drills like those referred to in the previous section provide useful, confidence-boosting preliminary activities, as do pole climbing and vaulting the 'widening stream'.

Riding down

1.   Use a long jump pit as a landing area. Stand on a raised take-off such as a gymnastics

47–9 Plant and take-off drills

box or steeplechase barrier, keeping the feet in line and the left foot forward. Hold the pole vertically in front of you with its lower end in the sand but close to the base of whatever you are standing on. Your right hand should be on top, just above eye level. Hands should be about 60 cm apart with the knuckles facing away from you.

2.   Push forwards over your front foot and swing to the ground *with* the pole, passing to the right side of it as you do so. Land with your feet side by side. Don't let go of the pole until you have landed safely (photographs 50–4).

3.   Repeat, trying to land your feet as far forward as possible at each attempt. As confidence improves, place a low, metre-high elastic bar half-way between take-off and landing and go over it. This will make you lift your hips forward as you clear it. Continue to hold on to the pole until in contact with the sand.

4.   Gradually raise the bar while moving it closer. Keep pressing the hips forwards and continue landing on two feet. Maintain a tight hold on the pole until you land.

5.   Remove the raised take-off. Pace out a 'giant' eight-stride approach (as for beginners in the other jumps). Toe the start-mark with the left foot while holding the pole as explained in the section on the approach. Run eight strides then plant and swing past the pole into the pit as you did when riding down. Ride for distance without a bar, then introduce the elastic bar as before.

6.   When confident of what you are doing, transfer to the pole vault bed and do exactly the same, but this time plant into the box and land on the bed, facing forwards with your feet together.

7.   Introduce an elastic bar one metre above the height of the bed. Vault first for distance, then for height, bringing the stands closer to the box as the bar is raised.

At this stage you are vaulting properly and can truly consider yourself a pole vaulter. Don't forget to maintain space between yourself and the pole during the plant, the take-off and the rock-back.

48

49

50–4 Riding down exercise for beginners

THE THROWS

Although throwing events tend to be the preserve of larger athletes, it is still possible for the smaller competitor to achieve some significance, especially in javelin and hammer. Smaller athletes can also participate very competitively in junior or women's competitions, since in these events the implements are smaller and lighter.

Although throwing events lack the immediacy of the track events, many people experience excitement at the sight of a really long throw, especially when the implement as it were takes off and flies. The problem lies in translating the awe that is felt into interest, understanding and enthusiasm. To throw a long way takes many hours, days and even years of diligent practice. To teach someone to throw well demands a lifetime of accumulated experience. Thus the

question is how can we help the 'man in the street' or the endurance fanatic to gain just a little insight into the fascination of these events so that they can be promoted more effectively?

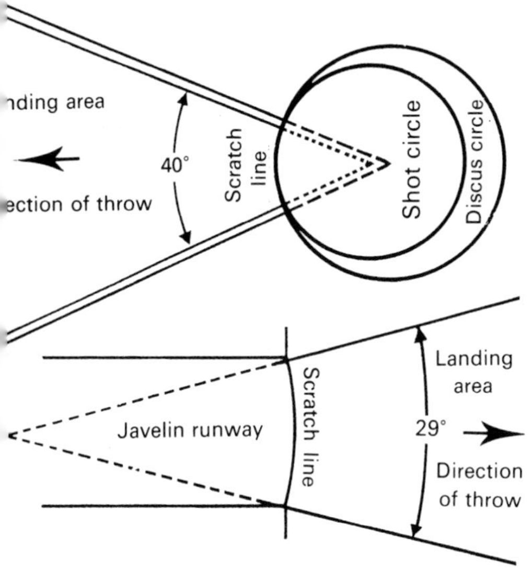

Despite this general lack of understanding throwing is easy to introduce and enjoy, even at very lowly levels of ability. One does not have to be an Olympic champion before one can derive satisfaction from involvement or motivation from improvement. In any of the four throwing disciplines such experiences are possible at one's second attempt.

The shot, the discus and the hammer are all thrown from a circle into a 40° landing sector. Any flat surface will provide a suitable platform from which to throw, but a hard one such as concrete is best. Shot and hammer circles must be of 2.135 m internal diameter, while discus circles are a little larger, measuring 2.5 m across.

The javelin is a little different. It is thrown from a runway 4 m wide with a maximum length of 36.5 m. The landing sector is enclosed by the extended radii of the 'scratch' line or baseline from behind which the implement is thrown. It encloses a segment of approximately 29°. The 'scratch' line is the arc of a circle of 8 m radius, joining the parallel sidelines of the runway where they border upon the landing sector.

Weight and speed

Reference has already been made to the fact that lighter implements permit women and younger athletes to compete at strength levels more appropriate to them. The competition specifications of implements, including their weight, are internationally standardised for adults. Modifications made to cater for the

Fig 4 Throws delivery and landing areas

special needs of adolescents differ slightly from country to country. Consult your national federation for details.

In cases where these adjustments still do not accommodate the physical capacity of an individual (i.e. for the very young, or the very small) it is essential that appropriate accommodation is made. The coach or the teacher must improvise so that the weight of the implement matches the ability of the thrower. Additionally, light implements permit the thrower to attain high release velocities, and so become competent at such levels of activity. Moreover, the capacity to perform in this manner as adults is founded on sound speed practice as youngsters.

Likewise, the acceptance of lightweight competition grades for adult athletes who are not of international class has great merit. Such a move would enable ordinary people to become more involved in throwing, thus increasing its popularity instead of perpetuating its exclusivity.

The fundamentals of technique

Distance is the product of speed of release and angle of release. Throwers greatly affect the speed of release by the way in which they summate their energies and channel them into the implement. In order to optimise the release angle, the shot and the hammer must be thrown at between 41° and 43° to the horizontal. The javelin and the discus, because they are influenced by wind speed and direction, need to be launched at lower angles, ranging down to about 30°.

The principles of effective throwing are:

- to apply force over as long a range or distance as possible
- to use legs and hips at the beginning of the delivery action in order to bring this about
- to use the arms both late and fast (almost as an afterthought)
- to keep the feet on the ground until after the implement has been released
- to brace the non-throwing side against the throwing action
- to start slowly and finish fast.

Balance is also important in bringing these things about, especially in the rotational throws. Imbalance is most apparent at the moment of release or just after, but it begins at the very earliest stages of the throw. It is here, at the source, that corrections are best made.

Safety

Safety must have a high priority in throwing. Unlike the jumps, where lack of care or foresight only endangers the performer, throwers put many others at risk if they behave in an irresponsible manner. For that reason the following general rules must be followed in a strictly disciplined way:

- never throw towards anyone
- always look to see that the landing sector is clear before throwing
- ensure that those people who need to be near the thrower are watching while each throw is made
- when throwing as part of a group you should all throw and then all collect together.

Additional rules relating to individual throwing events are covered in the relevant safety sections.

Without recourse to a cage, simultaneous throwing can provide an acceptable way of accommodating large groups of throwers, provided that individuals are adequately spaced, and those in charge are both competent and alert. Because of their rotational nature discus and hammer need more safety space than shot put or javelin.

Left-handers

The same problems apply for left-handed throwers as for their pole vaulting counterparts, pose problems for author and reader alike. The four throws chapters thus use the same convention as the pole vault chapter, and underlined instructions will need to be transposed by left-handers.

SHOT PUT

It is advantageous for shot putters to be both tall and heavy. They need to be tall so that they can release the shot from the highest possible launch pad, and heavy in order to provide a stable base from which to deliver it. Shot putters are thus the battleships of the athletic world.

Despite the need to be large, shot putters must also be quick. We already know that speed has a great influence upon how far the shot will travel, and it is important for both the coach and the athlete to keep this fact constantly in mind.

Safety

Shot put circles should have a wooden stop-board at the rim, adjacent to the landing sector. Its purpose is to enable throwers to check their forward momentum after release by placing their leading foot against its inner edge. Stop-boards are not essential for training, and they do represent a potential source of injury.

Provided that the main safety rules outlined at the beginning of this section are followed, the shot put is not very dangerous.

Equipment

Special shot put shoes, which are modified training shoes, can be obtained, but they are a luxury for all but the best throwers. Training shoes, tennis shoes or sneakers are more than adequate, and they have the added advantage of being much cheaper.

Special types of shot which do not damage the floor have been developed for use indoors.

They have either leather or plastic shells, and are filled with a mixture of sand and lead shot. They are very useful in cold climates during winter. They can be quite safely improvised by encasing an appropriate amount of loose lead shot in an old nylon stocking, tying it repeatedly and finally covering the whole thing again with an old woollen sock. Rounded stones collected from the sea-shore or river bed can also be used safely.

A towel is very useful when training or competing in the rain. In very cold weather conditions a bucket of hot water will keep the shot warm, and make training more pleasant.

Hold

Because the shot is 'put' or pushed, as distinct from being thrown, the rules demand that it is held against the neck under the chin, and not taken behind the line of the shoulders. These requirements dictate how it is held.

The shot should rest on the middle three fingers of the throwing hand, supported on either side by the thumb and the little finger. It should be pressed into the base of the neck on the side of the throwing arm (photograph 55) and kept there until the arm is brought into play as the final part of the throw.

The thrower should ensure that it stays clear of the palm of the hand throughout the course of the throw – hence the adage that a good shot putter has a 'clean palm and a dirty neck'.

Starting the throw

In both the conventional, linear style of throwing and the less conventional rotational

55 How to hold the shot

56 For the linear method of shot putting the athlete stays low with the weight on the rear foot

style, the thrower begins by standing at the back of the circle, facing away from the landing sector. Right-handed, conventional throwers will stand with the feet in line, close together, and the right toe tucked up against the circle rim. Rotational throwers will place the feet astride, shoulder width apart, and the toes of both feet will touch or press close to the circle rim.

The shot is placed to the base of the neck and kept there.

Building momentum

Initial momentum is created when the thrower moves from the back of the circle into the pre-delivery position at the front. This movement is generally referred to as the shift or the glide. Throwers using the linear or 'O'Brien' style achieve this by means of a low hop on their right leg, at the end of which the foot should have moved to a position at the centre

of the circle (or just beyond it) and turned anticlockwise through 70° or 80°. Meanwhile the torso should stay low but quite passive, and the shoulders and the hips should remain facing the rear. If successful this enables the thrower to work on the shot over a longer range in the delivery position. It is a bad fault to permit the shoulders and the hips to 'open out' towards the front of the circle as the shift is made.

Some throwers drop into the shift from an erect starting position, while others commence from a low crouch.

The left foot should stay close to the ground during the shift and remain inactive, leaving all the action to the right foot.

Rotational putters start by twisting anticlockwise on the balls of both feet. When they can see the front of the circle the right foot is lifted and taken around ahead of the left to its new position at the centre of the circle. The left foot leaves the ground just before the right foot lands, and as the thrower continues to rotate about the vertical axis it moves towards the delivery position at the front of the circle. One and a quarter turns are thus completed.

Although the movement is akin to that of the discus thrower, because the circle is smaller rotational putters cannot express themselves in quite as free a manner as discus throwers.

57 During the shift phase the athlete drives to the centre of the circle, keeping low

58 The shoulder axis is kept closed while the hip axis opens

59 The athlete thrusts hard with the rear leg

60 The athlete reaches out well beyond the stop-board when releasing the shot

61 and 62 (right)   **For the start of the rotational throw, both feet are kept close to the rim**

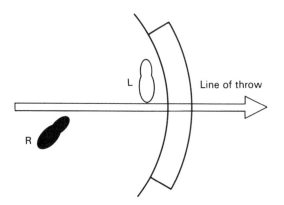

63 The athlete's weight is kept over the left leg during the entry phase

The shift must be tightly controlled, with the right foot landing at the centre and the right hip dominating the movement. It helps if rotational putters keep their weight distributed to their left, especially during the movement around the left foot at the back of the circle.

Pre-delivery

The key points of the pre-delivery position, when the thrower arrives at the centre of the circle, are that:

■ the thrower's weight acts through the right foot
■ the left leg is extended towards the stop-board
■ the hips are pressed towards the rear of the circle
■ the feet are offset either side of the line of throw (see figure 5)
■ the right hip is pressed ahead of the shot.

Fig 5   Offset feet at the pre-delivery

Note that the effect of extending the left leg to the stop-board and pressing the hips rearwards, is to produce what looks like a straight line silhouette through the left leg when viewed from the side. Such is the sort of picture for which coaches and teachers should be looking.

It is important to remember that the position through which the thrower passes should not be posed, but rather should be an active one.

64 During the turn the athlete runs around the left leg

65 The right foot moves to the centre of the circle while the left knee closes to the right

66 The left foot is placed down early

67 The right elbow is high as the shot is released

Also the right and left feet do not land simultaneously; the right lands slightly before the left, and a weight transfer from rear to front is executed which continues into the delivery itself.

Delivery

The fundamentals of the delivery action are common to both styles of throwing. It commences with a leg drive, directed forwards then upwards, which is continued through the hip and the torso, and finally progresses through the shoulder, the throwing arm, and the wrist.

The linear thrower will tend to use a wider stance (so that the right leg dominates more) and to work against a braced left leg and left side. However, some throwers, particularly in America, prefer to adopt a narrower stance and work through both legs. Those using a wide base emphasise horizontal leg drive, while those working from a narrower base exaggerate the vertical component. All rotational throwers work from a narrow base. The active right leg will keep its hip ahead of the shot so that the hips come round to the front before the torso, and the torso before the shoulders. The thrower thus unwinds as the movement progresses.

The action of the arms should retard this process, and in this respect the action of the left arm is of particular importance. Swung laterally at shoulder level, it will tend to open up the shoulder axis prematurely. Folded close to the head with high elbow, it will not have the same effect, but will assist the overriding need to keep the shoulders closed for as long as possible.

In rotational throwing, lateral use of the left arm at the beginning of the turn assists balance and stability. Having begun in the lateral plane it tends to remain there.

The throwing arm should be brought into the action late and fast. It should sequentially follow the actions of the trunk and the shoulders, almost as an afterthought. It begins as a 'punch' from the shoulder and ends as a 'flip' of the wrist. However, it is important that the elbow is kept high in order to effectively transmit power

as it extends along the 41° projection path of the shot.

The notion of the high throwing elbow is important throughout the rotational style. It enables the shot to be kept close to the neck when rotational forces are tending to pull it away. Similarly, at release it is important for the left side to be stopped or blocked so that rotation is halted and angular momentum is translated into linear velocity.

Two further principles are of importance. Firstly, the thrower should try to remain in contact with the shot for as long as possible (right out beyond the stop-board), and secondly, both feet should stay in firm contact with the circle until after the shot has been thrown.

Recovery

After a well balanced throw, recovery will happen naturally and throwers will have the following range of options open to them:

- to stand and watch the shot land
- to slightly lower the body and quickly reverse the foot positions
- to rotate around the left foot back to the centre of the circle.

Aids to training

Variations on the standing throw which are suitable for improving both basic strength and technique are the overhead throw, the chest throw, and the frontal standing shot put. All are made from a straddle stance.

Standing throws represent a very popular means of practising the delivery action. The common practice is to stand at the stop-board and step back to the centre before making the throw. However, this action is the exact reverse of what actually happens when a proper throw is made. The correct action can be simulated by starting at the centre of the circle and then stepping forward into the throw with the left foot.

To practise the delivery in the rotational style

the thrower must stand at the back of the circle, facing forwards, then place the right foot at its centre (doing so makes the thrower face the 'closed' side of the action). This is the starting position. The movement is commenced by turning the shoulders clockwise before 'rebounding' and pivoting anticlockwise around the right foot. The left foot is brought round into position at the front of the circle. The lifting, blocking action then follows.

Learning

The most effective way to learn to shot put is to begin with the delivery and then work progressively back to the shift.

1.   Chest-pass a football or a basketball to a coach or a partner. Make sure that even pressure is applied down both arms as the throw is made.

2.   Adopt an in-line foot placement with the left foot forward. Throw the ball to drive your partner backwards. As this happens you will have to throw the ball higher in order to make the distance. Continue to apply even pressure down both arms.

3.   Turn the chest to the right before making the throw. Continue to hold the ball at the chest and apply pressure down both arms. The chest and the hips will have to be turned to the front as the throw is made.

4.   Take the left hand away at the very last moment.

5.   Substitute a light shot for the ball, and hold it one-handed at the neck in the proper manner.

6.   Adjust your foot placement, checking that the front foot is offset. Make sure that you start with your weight on your right foot, and emphasise the right leg/hip drive as the throw is made.

Having perfected the standing throw it is time to move on to learning the shift. As already explained, the shift of the linear throw is essentially a hop, and is best learned in the following manner.

7.   Move the starting position one foot nearer the rear of the circle.

8.   Take your weight on your right foot, lifting the left foot just clear of the ground as you do so. Do a tiny, low, truncated hop into the delivery position, then throw. Don't forget to turn the rear foot as it moves.

9.   Gradually move your starting position further towards the back of the circle as ability and confidence improve. Push more strongly from the hopping leg at each stage of the progression.

There are no preparatory lead-ins to rotational putting. Adopt a slight sitting position at the back of the circle. Hold the shot tightly under the chin, and rotate around your left foot as described before. The movement can also be practised without the shot. Seek good balance throughout.

Discus

This event is very much the preserve of tall, rangy athletes, favouring men over 1.88 m (6 ft 2 in) and women over 1.78 m (5 ft 10 in). Long arms, proportional to height, are an added advantage. Like shot putters, discus throwers need to be explosive, and possess a well developed sense of balance.

Safety

Being a rotational, slinging event, the discus is much more dangerous than either the shot put or the javelin. The hold is a light one, making it easy for the discus to slip unexpectedly from the grasp. Great care must therefore be taken, and whenever possible, the use of safety nets is strongly advised. If this is not possible and people have to practise in groups, then great care must be taken, with each individual thrower spaced well away from the next. This is because the discus leaves the hand across the forefinger and tends to slice away to the throwing side if things do go wrong, thus endangering nearby throwers on that side.

Wet weather will increase the chances of the discus slipping prematurely from the hand, and also the likelihood of it skidding quite a way when it lands. Drying the discus with a towel before each throw will improve grip and control during the throw itself.

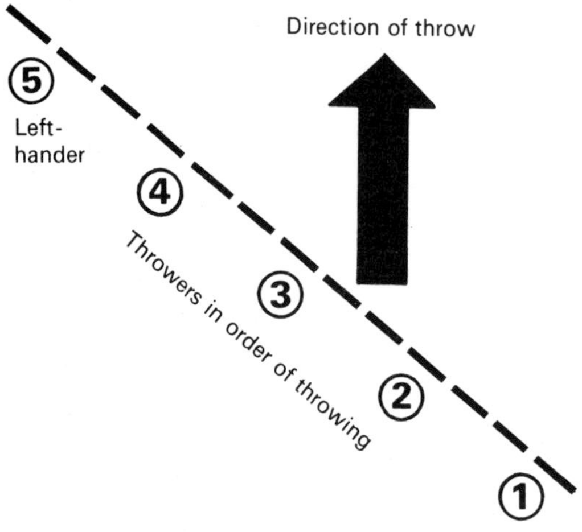

Equipment

Special discus shoes with soles which are curved at the edges are helpful to good quality throwers. Training or tennis shoes offer an adequate, cheaper alternative for those of lesser ability.

A towel is useful for drying the discus when throwing in wet weather, plus Venice turpentine or a similar adhesive substance for improving grip.

Solid rubber discuses are available, and these are particularly useful for indoor practice, net practice or bad weather.

Hold

The discus is held loosely in the palm of the hand, with the fingers spread and their end joints curled over the rim (see photograph 68). It should not be gripped.

When learning to throw, it is best to hold the discus at the left shoulder, supporting it on a platform formed by the fingers of the left hand, with the right hand on top (photograph 69). The discus is taken from this platform and returned to it during each preliminary swing.

Direction of throw

(5) Left-hander
(4)
Throwers in order of throwing
(3)
(2)
(1)

Fig 6   The safe organisation of a throwing group

68 Learning to hold the discus

Starting the throw

The experienced thrower will stand in a straddle position at the rear of the circle, facing away from the landing sector, with the feet shoulder width apart and the toes just touching the inside of the circle rim. Beginners will need to compromise this position (see pages 55–6).

The discus is held in the right hand before being taken across the body on an extended arm in a sweeping action, to a position behind the right shoulder, the torso twisting to the right as it does so. This movement is referred to as the 'swing', or the 'preliminary swing'. Only one is necessary. As the swing occurs the thrower's weight is shifted on to the right leg.

Building momentum

The first movement after the swing must be a shift of weight from the right leg on to, and around, the left, as both feet pivot anticlockwise on the ball of the foot. This is accompanied by an outwards rotation of both the left knee and the torso. An extended left arm assists balance,

69 The left hand forms a platform at the start of the swing

70 and 71 (right)   **It is important not to take the discus too far back during the swing**

while the right arm, holding the discus, trails the action.

Both feet stay in contact with the circle until the thrower is able to comfortably see the landing area. The right foot is then lifted and taken actively around the left in a high, swinging action, before being grounded at the centre of the circle. The left foot pushes strongly against the ground as the right foot passes it before it, too, breaks contact. Thus the right leg creates rotation, while the left drives the thrower forwards.

There is a brief period of flight when the thrower is completely off the ground.

Pre-delivery

The right foot must land on the ball of the foot so that both it and the thrower can continue to rotate. It is also important that the right foot should remain active. While this is happening the left leg closes to the mid-line (the direction of the throw in the sagittal plane) and extends towards the front of the circle, coming to

ground slightly offset to the left of the line of throw. Indeed both feet should finish in much the same position as those of the shot putter.

If the left leg doesn't close to the mid-line but is allowed to sweep into position through a wide arc, it will be late in getting to the front of the circle, thus disturbing both the timing and the range of the delivery action.

The arm holding the discus must always be behind the shoulder axis and behind the movement of the thrower around his vertical axis until the final flinging action. It must be fully extended in order to maximise the radius of the path of the discus around the vertical axis.

The key points of the final pre-delivery position into which the thrower settles at the end of this part of the throw are almost identical with those described for shot put (page 46), except that the discus and the throwing arm are extended behind the right shoulder above hip height. (If one imagines the circle to be a clock face aligned so that 12 o'clock is positioned at the front of the circle on the line of throw then the arm is extended to 10 o'clock.)

72 Weight should be kept over the left leg for the entry

73 The athlete runs ahead of the discus for the turn

74 The right foot is placed near the centre and keeps turning

75 Great use should be made of the hips during delivery

76 and 77 (right) **Both feet are kept on the ground until the discus has been released**

Delivery

This part of the throw is dominated by the right leg. A forward thrust is added to its active rotation, which has the effect of driving the right hip to the front, and transferring the body-weight on to the front leg. The torso takes up the action of the hips, and turns to face the front as the right leg completes its drive. During the final part of the drive, lift is added to thrust. As in shot put, this is accomplished against a braced left side. Meanwhile, the right arm remains long, relaxed and passive, trailing the action of the leg and the trunk until the final moments of the throw, when it too is actively employed in a slinging, lifting action.

Throughout the action it is vital that the discus is kept well away from the thrower's body (which provides the axis of rotation). Also the wrist must press forwards, ahead of the discus, to ensure that it rolls across the forefinger and out of the front of the hand.

The left arm is generally carried wider throughout the throw than for shot put in order to aid stability. Great care needs to be exercised to ensure that overzealousness during delivery doesn't cause the chest to open prematurely to the front.

Recovery

Residual rotation will make it more difficult for discus throwers to end the throw well balanced, compared to shot putters. It will also be harder for them to retain foot contact throughout the release and afterwards, thus making it more likely that they will use a more active form of recovery.

The recovery is often effected by changing the position of the feet with a little jump (active reverse), followed by a continuing pivot around the new front foot and a lateral movement of the free leg and the torso. Alternatively, it can be effected by lifting the right foot and spinning around the left, the torso remaining vertical. The active reverse is thought to help to increase the range over which the discus is worked at the front of the circle, while the main drawback of the spin recovery is that it encourages premature lifting of the rear foot, and thereby a reduction in release velocity.

Flight

In flight the discus will rotate in a clockwise direction. If it doesn't, check to see that it is coming out of the front of the hand. Its attitude should be quite flat so that it presents its rim to the air and cuts through it, creating lift like an aircraft's wing.

Aids to training

The standing throw provides the basis of the event and the basis of practice. As in shot put, there is equal value in stepping back from a starting position at the front of the circle, and in stepping forwards from a starting position at the centre of the circle.

The 'running front turn' is useful as a training drill and as a method of teaching the event. Begin the turn from the position shown in photograph 78, and emphasise the forwards nature of the movement rather than the rotational one. It is initially easier if the preliminary arm/discus movements are made vertically, like a clock pendulum, on the right-hand side of the thrower, with the thrower moving forward in time with the arm. Later modifications of this drill can include the use of lateral throwing arm movements, and the adoption of a side-on stance by turning either the right foot, or both feet, clockwise through 90°.

The practice for shot put described on page 49, involving a 'half-turn' made around the right foot, is very appropriate for discus. A walking version of this, done without the discus, is also useful for practising the tight left leg action at the end of the turn.

Throwing into indoor nets is a beneficial exercise since it enables the thrower to concentrate on the 'feel' of the event to the exclusion of all else. However, this mustn't be overdone otherwise the experience of the whole throw can be lost.

78 Starting position for the 'running front turn'

Learning

The following sequence represents a sound method of introducing the throw to beginners.

1.   Stand facing the landing area with your feet in line, the left foot forward and the discus, correctly held, hanging loosely by your right hip. Swing the discus rhythmically forwards and backwards, transferring your body-weight *with* it as you do so. Release the discus going forwards so that it lands vertically on its edge.
2.   Place a target on the ground, straight ahead, about 20 m away. Take up a side-on stance, with the left shoulder pointing to the target, the feet at 90° to the line of throw, and the left foot slightly offset in the proper manner. Support and hold the discus by the left shoulder (photograph 69). Withdraw it laterally on an extended arm, and sling it so that it flies horizontally, ricocheting from the ground by the target. Move the target further away as you improve, and try to lift the discus over it. The discus must continue to fly horizontally.

3.   When you have gained in confidence shift your weight on to the right foot as the discus is swung back, then use the right leg to drive its hip forwards as the throw is made. Ensure that both feet twist towards the direction of throw. Work hard to master the feel of this action.

4.   Ensure that you finish high over your front foot, with the shoulders level and the feet firmly on the ground at the moment of release.

When the standing throw has been learned well the thrower will be ready to add the turn. The following progression is an appropriate way of introducing this. The early stages are best done across a running track without a discus.

5.   Adopt the starting position of the 'running front turn' (photograph 78) with the front foot toeing one of the lane lines.

6.   Rock across the left foot, jumping forwards to land right–left with your right foot on the next lane line, and the left beyond it.

7.   Repeat point 6, but under an outstretched right arm.

8.   Repeat point 7, but this time make an anticlockwise turn in the air to land with both feet pointing away from the direction in which you were moving. Keep the outstretched arm facing in its original direction. This stage may initially prove a little awkward for some.

9.   Repeat point 8, preceded by a swinging right arm, timing the forward drive so that it coincides with the arm's swing to shoulder height, ahead of the body.

10.   Repeat point 9, pause on landing with the swinging arm drawn back behind the shoulder, then simulate a controlled standing throw as in point 3.

11.   Throw a discus from the circle, repeating point 10 in a continuous, active manner. The starting position is outside the circle (see photograph 78).

Obviously, this way of throwing is not permitted in competition. It can be suitably modified by bringing the feet very close together and standing so that the back foot is just inside and clear of the rim.

Further modifications leading to the use of a 'back to landing sector' stance can be made by means of successive 45° progressions of the body and the feet, turning clockwise away from the landing sector until the desired starting position is reached.

As the more extreme positions are reached it becomes imperative that the thrower pivots on both feet to his left as the turn is begun.

JAVELIN

The practitioners of the javelin event are quite different from other throwers. Also, although javelin is similar to shot put in that it is a straight line event, it is unique among the throws in being performed from a runway. Javelin probably has more in common with horizontal jumps in terms of the event structure, and with combined events in terms of the physical characteristics of its practitioners and its training regime.

Safety

Javelins are pointed and thus penetrate whatever they hit. They are the most dangerous of the athletic implements, and great care is necessary when using them. As well as the general safety rules which apply to throwing, the following additional safeguards must be observed.

1. The javelin must always be held safely when not being thrown (i.e. vertically, point-down in front of the carrier).
2. When preparing to throw, both the thrower and those awaiting their turn must be conscious of the danger which the sharp tail of the javelin represents and act accordingly.
3. Never run while carrying a javelin or when retrieving it.
4. The javelin is always pushed upright before being drawn from the ground.

Equipment

Like high jumpers, javelin throwers land on their heels during the final strides of the approach run. Thus in order to stop them from slipping they need shoes with spikes in the heel which are longer than those permitted for other events. The shoes also need to be high-sided to give greater lateral support. Such shoes are understandably quite expensive. They do, however, constitute a sensible personal safety precaution, making them essential to all those who are serious about the event.

As in the discus event, the javelin thrower will need a towel with which to dry the implement during wet weather, and also some gripping aid, for example Venice turpentine or Photo-mount.

The wearing of special elastic supports for the back and the elbow of the throwing arm is becoming more popular among javelin throwers as a means of preventing injury, rather than just as a post-injury cure.

Hold

The 'split-finger' or 'claw' grip (photograph 79) is a good introduction to the event because it teaches throwers to support the implement with the throwing hand, and encourages them to keep the throwing arm and the elbow in an injury-free position, close to the body.

The thumb and second finger or 'Finnish' method (photograph 80) is most popular among top-class throwers because the placement of the index finger along the shaft of the javelin increases its rate of spin, and thus its stability, in flight. Beginners can misunderstand all too easily, placing the index finger under the shaft with disastrous results.

The third method of gripping the javelin (photograph 81) is seldom, if ever, used except by the uninitiated.

79 The 'split finger' or 'claw' grip for javelin

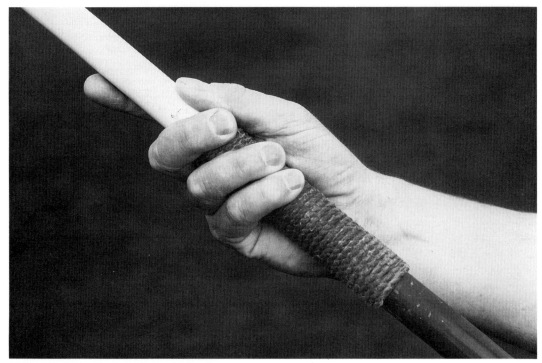

80 The 'Finnish' method of gripping the javelin

81 The thumb and first finger or 'darts' grip

Starting the throw

This section could just as easily be entitled 'The approach' since javelin throwers begin their throw with an approach run similar to that of a jumper.

The run will be between 7 and 13 strides long, measured from a release position some 2 m (6 ft) behind the scratch (or throw) line, depending upon ability. This 'free' space is necessary in order to give the thrower room in which to stop after release without stepping on to, or over, the scratch line, and thus infringing the rules.

The natural rhythm of the delivery sequence is a three-stride one. Therefore, its structure goes against the general runway format established on page 9. Javelin throwers stand with their right foot at the start-mark. This ensures that the first running stride is made with the left foot, over which the throw is then made.

The javelin should be held high over the right shoulder. Whether it is held horizontally, angled so that it points slightly upwards, or downwards is a matter of personal preference and trial and error. The height at which the javelin is held is also a matter of personal taste. However, low carries tend to lead eventually to injury of the throwing elbow. Wherever it is held it should permit the palm of the hand to face upwards and the elbow to be placed underneath.

Building momentum

The approach run should be made in an easy, balanced manner, keeping the javelin correctly aligned along the direction and plane of the throw, and the arm working like a car's suspension to give it a smooth ride. As the left foot moves forward at the beginning of the fifth stride from delivery, the throwing arm should commence its withdrawal, which is completed before the end of the next stride. The shoulders turn to the right at the same time.

The withdrawal is an important part of the throw. It may be either a straight push back or an up-and-backwards extension of the arm

82 The athlete runs ahead of the javelin during the 'withdrawal stride'

supporting the implement. It should occur sufficiently far from delivery to enable the thrower to settle the javelin into its final alignment, but not so far as to constitute a carrying problem – hence the five stride convention which is the best available compromise.

Good throwers will concentrate on running forwards ahead of the javelin in order to minimise any reduction in its accumulated forward momentum. The left foot should be starting to turn slightly to its right when it lands.

Pre-delivery

The penultimate stride provides one of the keys to the throw. The right foot is moved ahead of the left foot and the body's vertical axis in what

amounts to a small jump. It thus lands heel first ahead of the body, tilting the vertical axis backwards in doing so (see photographs 82–9). The thrower should not lean back for the tilt.

While airborne the left leg is brought forward alongside the right so that it is in position, ready to be grounded, as soon as the right foot has made contact. At the same time the right foot should point at 45° to the line of the throw on landing.

The throwing hand should remain high, with the palm facing upwards. Leaving the arm slightly flexed at the elbow joint will help novices to avoid dropping the arm, which would cause them to present the javelin at too steep a delivery angle. Other possible contributors to this bad fault are dropping the hand at the wrist joint (as in the overhead smash in badminton or tennis), or letting go of the grip with the third and fourth fingers.

83 and 84 Throughout the second and third strides the athlete keeps the throwing arm high

85 The right foot is taken ahead of the left

Delivery

The thrower will pass very quickly over the right foot on to the left, during which time many things have to happen. As the thrower's body-weight moves over and beyond the right foot he will arrive in a position from which he can push strongly, driving the hips forwards and around to the front in the process. The torso and the shoulders follow in a manner similar to that of the shot putter and this particular phase must be well underway before the left foot has landed. Timing is critical, and yet it is all over almost before one knows it. The front foot should point in the direction of the throw when it finally meets the ground. It should be slightly offset to its own side of the line of the throw.

The throwing arm must not be brought into the action until the very last moment, when all other body parts have played their part. The torso and shoulder rotation draws the arm forwards, ensuring that as it leads the flailing action of the arm, the elbow begins to move into a high position near the right ear. This final action should be faster than any which preceded it, with the hand moving upwards as well as forwards along the path to be followed eventually by the javelin. Arms which are naturally fast are essential for throwing a long way.

As the thrower passes over the left leg during the final moments of the delivery, the leg braces against the action, thus adding a final vertical component.

86 The athlete lands on a passive right leg and grounds the left one quickly

87 The athlete drives the right hip forwards

**88 and 89 The elbow
leads in the delivery
stage for javelin**

89

Recovery

The horizontal velocity which remains after release should be sufficient to carry the thrower forwards beyond the front leg at delivery. It is for this reason that 'free' space is needed between delivery and the scratch line.

When the right leg lands in the follow-through stride the thrower should resist forward momentum with it as strongly as possible. A slight lowering of the hips will help this process. Make sure, even at this stage, that the shoulders are level when facing the landing sector, and that the whole process is balanced.

Aids to training

Balls for throwing are an important aid for the javelin thrower. It is possible to use anything from basketballs or large medicine balls to baseballs, softballs, hockey balls, cricket balls or specially made plastic covered 'slingballs'. The latter are available from reputable athletics suppliers in weights ranging from 150 g up to the lighter varieties of indoor shot.

By carefully selecting the right resistance, these balls can be thrown into nets or against walls to improve speed, strength or endurance. While those with soft centres (the slingballs) afford the best protection for costly flooring or for participants, they do not rebound from walls and are thus incapable of being used for fast repetition work.

It is possible to improvise by filling tennis balls with sand and lead shot and then re-sealing them with several layers of adhesive tape. Alternatively, you could simply use stones.

Learning

1. Grip the javelin in one of the ways described, preferably in the claw grip.
2. Stand in the starting position described earlier (that is left foot forward) and point the javelin at a target placed on the ground about 10m away.
3. Withdraw the javelin, keeping it lined up with the target. Throw the javelin to stick in the ground near the target. It should land pointing straight back between your eyes, like the javelin in the centre of photograph 90. The javelins on either side in the picture have landed incorrectly, and energy has been wasted. As such they are examples of wrongly channelled throwing.

90 The javelin in the centre is in the correct landing attitude

4.   Move back three large steps. Stand as in point 2 but with the right foot forward. Withdraw the javelin, then run three strides left–right–left and throw. Continue to throw at the same target and keep trying to get the javelin landing in correct alignment. The timing of the running steps should be 's–t–e–p . . . right/left or s–l–o–w . . . quick/quick'. Work to land on your heels, and move the right foot to land ahead of the body as described in the pre-delivery section.

5.   After withdrawal add two preliminary strides to make up a 5-stride sequence. The target can be gradually moved further away, or a new target can be selected (for example the top of a high tree or building, or an imaginary shelf in the sky which assures a 30° angle of throw). The aim should be to throw the javelin so that it is rifled out to 'sit' on the shelf or the high object. This prevents faulty anticipation and hence exaggeration of the javelin's rotation around its short axis.

6.   The next stage is to change the drill so that the javelin is withdrawn at the precise moment that the first step is taken, not before. In this way correct timing of the withdrawal is established.

7.   Finally, add blocks of either two or four strides, carrying the javelin over the throwing shoulder in order to produce a 7, 9, 11 or 13-stride approach run as required.

HAMMER

Although it is of some advantage for hammer throwers to be heavy like shot putters, they tend to be of shorter stature. Some of the best throwers in the world are currently less than 1.83 m (6 ft) tall. The event thus provides the ideal alternative for the shorter shot putter.

Hammer throwers need to be naturally strong. They are similar to weight-lifters in build and become more than capable lifters through training.

Safety

The perceived dangers of this event usually frighten teachers and club coaches into a policy of neglect. However the hammer is, in reality, no more dangerous than any other throwing event, and it can be introduced under the same conditions as apply for shot put, discus or javelin, provided that the standard safety precautions are carefully observed.

Admittedly, the hammer does cause more superficial damage to the landing area than other throwing events. However, if any turf damage is repaired by infilling with soil at the end of each throwing session, games pitches (other than hockey or cricket pitches) need not be rendered unusable by hammer practice.

Competition hammer wires are specially treated in order to prevent them from stretching, but this makes them rather brittle and liable to snap easily if they get a kink in them. Avoid using wires which are in such a condition. Fencing wire of No. 11 steel wire gauge is much more pliable, and is a safer substitute for training purposes.

The spindle around which the head of the hammer rotates can often become blocked by soil. This in turn can cause wires to break. It is a sensible precaution to check that the head turns freely before each throw. It is also prudent to keep spindles well oiled, and to store hammers in a hanging position so that the wire is kept straight.

It is important that those who must be close when throwing is in progress stand opposite the low point of the plane which the hammer follows when moving around the thrower. This is to the thrower's right, since the wire is most likely to snap when it is subjected to the greatest force, that is when the hammer approaches its low point in each revolution. If the wire should break in these circumstances, the hammer will fly off along the ground at a tangent, to the thrower's left, and missing those people correctly positioned in the process.

Where possible throw from a safety cage.

Equipment

Very capable hammer throwers need special throwing shoes with curved soles similar to those worn by discus throwers. Indeed this type of shoe was first designed with the needs of hammer throwers in mind. Flat, smooth-soled shoes such as plimsolls will suffice for less capable throwers.

Protection for the hand which is in direct contact with the hammer handle is essential. Special gloves can be purchased but an old heavy duty leather or rubber glove will do. Some throwers manage quite well by taping up their fingers with bandage or adhesive tape.

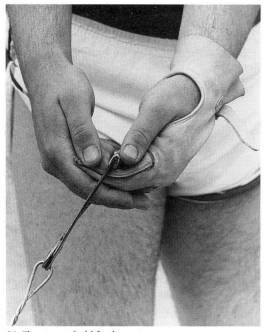

91 The correct hold for hammer

Hold

The hammer handle is held in the left hand, over which the right is then closed (photograph 91).

Starting the throw

The thrower takes up a position at the rear of the circle, facing away from the landing sector with the feet shoulder width apart, just as in the discus event. The hammer is placed on the right, with its head close by the little toe of the right foot. The handle is held directly above it, and the wire is fully extended.

From this position the hammer's head is moved anticlockwise across the front of the body, while the hands circle up and across the forehead before passing behind the head and back to their starting position. The hammer's head passes around and behind the thrower as they do so. This movement is referred to as the swing and most throwers perform either two or three of them. The swings are used to establish the hammer in its correct plane of movement (in

which its low point is in front of the thrower and its high point is to the rear), and to get it moving.

While this is happening the thrower should remain relaxed and balanced. The movement should be smooth and the thrower should transfer his weight from right to left, ahead of the movement of the hammer.

Beginners tend to turn their shoulders towards the hammer at its high point, after it has moved behind them. This should be avoided and the shoulders should remain facing the front, otherwise further minor difficulties will occur during later stages of the throw.

Building momentum

This is achieved by adding three (sometimes four) turns to the swings. The movement which links the swings to the turns is referred to as the entry. It begins when the hammer's head is at its high point, and ends just after it has passed the low point of the final swing. The thrower's weight must shift left as the hammer moves through the high point. At the same time the hips must begin to turn anticlockwise just ahead of the hammer. While this is happening quite complex tasks are demanded of the feet. They pivot simultaneously on the left heel and the right toe.

The timing of this movement is quite subtle. The thrower moves *with* the hammer as it passes the right foot, so that both hammer and right hip become as one and move together. Some anticipation of the action by the feet is necessary in order to get it right. The hips must press towards the hammer during the entry. Under no circumstances should they be permitted to 'pike' or move away from it.

The arms should remain long and passive throughout. The hands should not rise above hip level. Both feet continue turning, maintaining contact with the ground until the left foot points towards the landing area. Weight is then transferred on to the ball of the left foot, and the right foot leaves the ground. By now the hammer will have risen further, but the hands should still be below shoulder height.

Having been raised off the ground, the right

92 and 93 (right)   **The hammer throw begins with two or three relaxed swings**

94 The entry is made *with* the hammer

95 The arms are kept below shoulder height

96 The athlete is relaxed and takes the right leg ahead of the hammer

97 The right foot must be placed down early

98 and 99 (above left and right) **The hammer is lifted long and high for the delivery**

foot is taken around the turning thrower in a pumping action. Both the thrower and his right foot continue to turn around the common central axis which acts through the left foot. After one complete rotation the right foot finally comes to rest back in its starting position, having travelled one foot length towards the front of the circle. The first turn is thus completed. The turn is repeated twice more before delivering.

Four-turn throwing is a little different. The entry is made on the toes of both feet, the left heel remaining off the ground throughout the first turn. Subsequent turns are then made as described above.

Pre-delivery

As the turns progress the outward pull of the hammer will become greater and greater and the thrower will have to counteract this in some way. It is better to sit slightly (i.e. to lower one's centre of gravity) than to lean away from the hammer, although the latter is easier. Leaning away from the hammer will result in a complementary straightening of the left leg, and should be avoided. It can be corrected by trying to keep the upper body relaxed and upright, while permitting the shoulders to be pulled towards the hammer.

The turns should get tighter and tighter as the throw progresses, and the hips should move ahead of the hammer by the final turn so that the thrower 'leads' it. This is achieved by seeking ever earlier grounding of the right foot at the completion of each turn. If the hammer has been permitted to find its own path after entry, as it should, then the plane will get steeper and steeper as the turns progress.

Delivery

The final delivery position should be one in which the right foot lands ahead of the hammer with the hips leading. This makes it possible for force to be added to the hammer by means of a final two-leg lift. This will all happen so quickly

that the thrower will have little time in which to concentrate upon individual points of technique. Provided that the landing is good, and it has been possible to keep the weight over the left leg, things will happen almost automatically.

The delivery pull, if there is one, occurs downwards immediately after the high point has been reached at the end of the final turn. If the plane has steepened correctly through the turns the hammer's head will pass close to the body as it goes through the low point. Thereafter, the thrower should lift hard and high through both legs (photographs 98 and 99).

Recovery

A balanced delivery needs no recovery. Where balance is not perfect, lower the hips slightly and 'change feet' as in discus or shot put. Throwers possessing more residual rotation than this may need to continue to pivot on their left leg back to the centre of the circle.

Aids to training

Special skill training is mainly based upon differing combinations of swings and turns. Through repetition of these the thrower learns to recognise the particular feel and balance of differing parts of the throw. Such drills include:

■ one swing followed by one turn, repeated a number of times in succession
■ two swings followed by one turn, repeated as above
■ two swings followed by two turns, repeated
■ three swings followed by one or two turns, repeated
■ three swings followed by three turns.

Large numbers of swings are used to work on the skills of swinging, whereas fewer swings combined with more turns can be used to work on balance, and on the thrower's relationship to the hammer while turning.

Special strength training involves the throwing of hammers which are heavier than those used in competition. These are thrown on varying combinations of wire lengths, and can weigh as much as 10 kg. Very short, heavy hammers are good for developing delivery strength. Long, very heavy hammers tend to change the overall timing of the throw. For this reason one must be very careful about the frequency of such work.

Jumping activities are useful for developing the elastic properties of the legs.

Learning

The short hammer method described below is the best for use with groups of young throwers.

1.   First remove the wire from the hammer by untwisting it at both ends. Replace it with two 'D' shackles (photograph 100).
2.   Stand at the front of the circle, facing away from the direction of throw. Position the hammer just outside your right knee. Hold the handle correctly and heave it over your left shoulder. Work to keep the arms long and

straight, and the body-weight centred over the left leg. Finish in balance, facing the landing area. You will need to pivot on both feet to achieve this.
3.   Repeat point 2 but this time position the hammer outside your left knee, holding the handle only in your left hand. Lift the hammer in front of the chest before letting it drop to your right side (in pendulum fashion). Then insert the right hand and complete the throw.
4.   Take up a new position at the centre of the circle, with your weight acting through the ball of your left foot. Start as before but, when the hammer is by your right knee, do a discus-style jump-turn around that left foot before throwing. Make sure that you come out of the turn with the feet facing the rear of the circle – not towards the left side as in discus.
5.   At the next stage start the jump-turn by dropping on to the left heel before turning on it until the foot points towards the landing area (i.e. through 180°). Transfer your weight on to your left toe before completing the turn.
6.   Finally, keep your left foot in contact with the ground throughout, thereby ensuring that you complete the turn in the proper manner.

100 The 'short' hammer

Two and three turns can then be built, and the hammer lengthened gradually using nylon pulley cord of 227 kg breaking strain. When the hammer reaches its correct length you can re-insert the wire.

Constant practice of the skill of turning is vital to success. Until it is mastered your throwing will be greatly retarded. Ten minutes' 'homework' each day, both with and without the hammer, works wonders.

COMBINED EVENTS

Combined, or multi-event specialists come in all shapes and sizes, but they tend to be predominantly power athletes. They are the all-rounders of the sport, and although there is an 800 metre event in the women's competition and a 1,500 metre event in the men's there is really no place in heptathlon or decathlon for slight, middle-distance physiques. Also, the extra weight of the specialist thrower is counter-productive, given that so many of the individual disciplines involve running and jumping. The majority of participants are thus drawn from the ranks of those jumpers and sprinters who are slightly taller than average, and who have the added ability to absorb skills quickly.

Organisation

The main events in this group are heptathlon (seven events) for women, and decathlon (ten events) for men. Pentathlon, the original, five-discipline, ancient Greek contest from which the current events are derived, still survives, albeit in a changed form. It is now less popular than the longer versions, and is subject to some local interpretation as to its content. In some parts of the world special intermediate formats such as the octathlon (eight events) have been created in order to provide a progressive development of multi-event experience for growing youngsters.

Heptathlon and decathlon usually take place over two days, although it is possible for them to be compressed into one day should circumstances dictate. (This is more unusual in decathlon for very obvious reasons.)

The best performance attained as the result of a single attempt in running events, and three attempts in other events (accepting that high jump and vault are conducted as usual), is translated into points by reference to the IAAF Scoring Tables for men's and women's combined event competitions. Placement in the competition as a whole is determined by the total of the scores in each of the individual events. Thus it is possible to do poorly in one or two events yet win the competition overall.

Large numbers of competitors are accommodated by allocating them to heats for running events and competition pools for field events. All competition in each discipline must be completed before the next commences. Minimum rest periods between disciplines are prescribed.

Contestants are disqualified following three false starts in running events. This is more lenient than the corresponding rule for normal running events.

Competitions for junior athletes use hurdles and throwing implements appropriate for their particular age group. This may entail the compilation of special tables to accommodate any anomalies such as hurdle races over shorter distances.

Heptathlon

The events, in order, are 100 metres, high jump, shot put, and 200 metres on the first day, followed by long jump, javelin and 800 metres on the second. Although the correct order of events should be as listed, organisers are empowered to change it if they need to.

A small portion of the Scoring Tables for heptathlon is reproduced in table 1. Scores for hand-timed hurdles performances (accurate to one-tenth of a second) are listed in the

100 metre Hurdles		Shot Put		Long Jump		800 metres	
Seconds	Points	Metres	Points	Metres	Points	Minutes	Points
15.0	810	14.22	809	5.89	816	2:21.10	809
15.1	797	14.21	808	5.88	813	2:21.18	808
15.2	784	14.19	807	5.87	810	2:21.25	807
15.3	772	14.18	806	5.86	807	2:21.33	806
15.4	759	14.16	805	5.85	804	2:21.40	805
15.5	746	14.15	804	5.84	801	2:21.48	804
15.6	734	14.13	803	5.83	798	2:21.55	803
15.7	722	14.12	802	5.82	795	2:21.62	802
15.8	709	14.10	801	5.81	792	2:21.70	801
15.9	697	14.09	800	5.80	789	2:21.77	800
16.0	685	12.42	689	5.49	697	2:30.34	689
16.1	673	12.40	688	5.48	694	2:30.42	688
16.2	661	12.39	687	5.47	691	2:30.50	687
16.3	649	12.37	686	5.46	688	2:30.58	686
16.4	638	12.36	685	5.45	686	2:30.67	685
16.5	626	12.34	684	5.44	683	2:30.75	684
16.6	615	12.33	683	5.43	680	2:30.83	683
16.7	603	12.31	682	5.42	677	2:30.91	682
16.8	592	12.30	681	5.41	674	2:30.99	681
16.9	581	12.28	680	5.40	671	2:31.07	680
17.0	570	10.60	569	4.99	557	2:40.38	569
17.1	559	10.59	568	4.98	554	2:40.46	568
17.2	548	10.57	567	4.97	551	2:40.55	567
17.3	537	10.55	566	4.96	548	2:40.64	566
17.4	526	10.54	565	4.95	546	2:40.73	565
17.5	516	10.52	564	4.94	543	2:40.81	564
17.6	505	10.51	563	4.93	540	2:40.90	563
17.7	495	10.49	562	4.92	538	2:40.99	562
17.8	484	10.48	561	4.91	535	2:41.08	561
17.9	474	10.46	560	4.90	532	2:41.17	560
18.0	464	8.76	449	4.59	451	2:49.52	469
18.1	454	8.75	448	4.58	448	2:49.62	468
18.2	444	8.73	447	4.57	446	2:49.71	467
18.3	434	8.72	446	4.56	443	2:49.81	466
18.4	424	8.70	445	4.55	441	2:49.91	465
18.5	415	8.69	444	4.54	438	2:50.00	464
18.6	405	8.67	443	4.53	436	2:50.10	463
18.7	396	8.66	442	4.52	433	2:50.20	462
18.8	387	8.64	441	4.51	431	2:50.29	461
18.9	377	8.62	440	4.50	428	2:50.39	460

Table 1   Extracts from the heptathlon scoring tables

COMBINED EVENTS

	RUNNING EVENTS				JUMPING EVENTS			THROWING EVENTS		
Points	100 m	400 m	1500 m	Hurdles	High Jump	Long Jump	Pole Vault	Shot Put	Discus	Javelin
500		57.57	5:10.73	18.25		5.59		10.24	31.78	43.96
499	12.82	57.59	5:10.91	18.27				10.22	31.74	43.88
498		57.62	5:11.09	18.28		5.58	3.56	10.20	31.68	43.82
497	12.83	57.65	5:11.28	18.29				10.19	31.64	43.74
496		57.67	5:11.46	18.30	1.64	5.57	3.55	10.17	31.58	43.68
495	12.84	57.70	5:11.64	18.31				10.15	31.54	43.62
494	12.85	57.73	5:11.82	18.32		5.56		10.14	31.48	43.54
493		57.76	5:12.01	18.33			3.54	10.12	31.44	43.48
492	12.86	57.78	5:12.20	18.34		5.55		10.10	31.38	43.40
491		57.81	5:12.38	18.35				10.09	31.34	43.34
490	12.87	57.84	5:12.57	18.36		5.54	3.53	10.07	31.28	43.26
489		57.87	5:12.75	18.37				10.05	31.24	43.20
488	12.88	57.89	5:12.94	18.38	1.63		3.52	10.04	31.18	43.14
487	12.89	57.92	5:13.12	18.39		5.53		10.02	31.12	43.06
486		57.95	5:13.31	18.41				10.00	31.08	43.00
485	12.90	57.97	5:13.49	18.42		5.52	3.51	9.99	31.02	42.92
484		58.00	5:13.68	18.43				9.97	30.98	42.86
483	12.91	58.03	5:13.86	18.44		5.51		9.95	30.92	42.78
482		58.06	5:14.05	18.45			3.50	9.94	30.88	42.72
481	12.92	58.08	5:14.24	18.46		5.50		9.92	30.82	42.66
480	12.93	58.11	5:14.42	18.47	1.62		3.49	9.90	30.78	42.58
479		58.14	5:14.61	18.48		5.49		9.89	30.72	42.52
478	12.94	58.17	5:14.80	18.49				9.87	30.68	42.44
477		58.19	5:14.98	18.50		5.48	3.48	9.85	30.62	42.38
476	12.95	58.22	5:15.01	18.51				9.84	30.58	42.30
475	12.96	58.25	5:15.36	18.52		5.47	3.47	9.82	30.52	42.24
474		58.28	5:15.54	18.54				9.80	30.48	42.18
473	12.97	58.30	5:15.73	18.55		5.46		9.79	30.42	42.10
472		58.33	5:15.92	18.56	1.61		3.46	9.77	30.36	42.04
471	12.98	58.36	5:16.11	18.57		5.45		9.75	30.32	41.96
470	12.99	58.39	5:16.30	18.58				9.74	30.26	41.90
469		58.42	5:16.48	18.59		5.44	3.45	9.72	30.22	41.82
468	13.00	58.44	5:16.67	18.60				9.70	30.16	41.76
467		58.47	5:16.86	18.61		5.43	3.44	9.69	30.12	41.68
466	13.01	58.50	5:17.05	18.62				9.67	30.06	41.62
465		58.53	5:17.24	18.63		5.42		9.65	30.02	41.56
464	13.02	58.55	5:17.43	18.65	1.60		3.43	9.64	29.96	41.48
463	13.03	58.58	5:17.62	18.66		5.41		9.62	29.92	41.42
462		58.61	5:17.81	18.67			3.42	9.60	29.86	41.34
461	13.04	58.64	5:18.00	18.68		5.40		9.59	29.80	41.28
460		58.67	5:18.19	18.69				9.57	29.76	41.20
459	13.05	58.69	5:18.38	18.70		5.39	3.41	9.55	29.70	41.14
458	13.06	58.72	5:18.57	18.71				9.54	29.66	41.08
457		58.75	5:18.76	18.72	1.59	5.38	3.40	9.52	29.60	41.00
456	13.07	58.78	5:18.95	18.73				9.50	29.56	40.94
455		58.81	5:19.14	18.75		5.37		9.49	29.50	40.86
454	13.08	58.84	5:19.33	18.76			3.39	9.47	29.46	40.80
453	13.09	58.86	5:19.52	18.77		5.36		9.45	29.40	40.72
452		58.89	5:19.71	18.78				9.44	29.36	40.66
451	13.10	58.92	5:19.91	18.79		5.35	3.38	9.42	29.30	40.58
450		58.95	5:20.10	18.80				9.40	29.24	40.52

Table 2   Extracts from the decathlon scoring tables

left-hand column, while those for the other three events are listed alongside A consistent score of 500 points in all seven events will produce a total of 3,500 points, which approximates to average club standard. National standard requires a 5,500 plus total, while to be among the best in the world requires 6,500 plus. A good score in the heptathlon for under-17s would be 4,000 points, and 3,000 for under-15s in the pentathlon.

Decathlon

First day events include 100 metres, long jump, shot put, high jump and 400 metres. The second day consists of 110-metres hurdles, discus, pole vault, javelin and 1,500 metres. As in heptathlon, alterations to the order of events can be made.

Table 2 represents a sample section of the decathlon Scoring Tables. An average of 500 points per event will bring a total score of 5,000

		Hurdles	High Jump	Shot Put	200 metres
(a)	Performance needed to score:				
	1000 points	13.85 secs	1.82 m	17.07 m	23.80 secs
	750 points	15.71 secs	1.62 m	13.34 m	26.55 secs
	500 points	17.89 secs	1.39 m	9.55 m	29.75 secs
	250 points	20.66 secs	1.14 m	5.66 m	33.80 secs
(b)	Number of points gained by improvements of:	0.2 secs	5 cm	40 cm	0.5 secs
At 1000 point standard		28	64	27	48
At 750 point standard		25	59	27	42
At 500 point standard		21	53	26	35
At 250 point standard		15	45	25	26

		Long Jump	Javelin	800 metres
(a)	Performance needed to score:			
	1000 points	6.48 m	57.18 m	2 mins 07.63 secs
	750 points	5.67 m	44.28 m	2 mins 25.56 secs
	500 points	4.78 m	31.22 m	2 mins 46.60 secs
	250 points	3.74 m	17.88 m	3 mins 13.55 secs
(b)	Number of points gained by improvements of:	10 cm	2 m	1.5 secs
At 1000 point score		29	39	22
At 750 point score		27	38	19
At 500 point score		27	38	16
At 250 point score		22	37	11

Table 3   Shows (a) the performance required, and (b) the number of points gained by the given improvements in heptathlon at 1000; 750; 500 and 250 points standard

points, which is about club standard. National standard requires a total of 7,500 points, and world standard better than 8,700. A good score for under-20s would be 4,500 points, or 5,500 if using special Junior apparatus. For under-17s using special apparatus, 5,000 points would be equal to national standard.

Planning

The techniques of the field event elements of combined events have been well covered in the individual sections of this book. The reader will need to turn to *Skilful Track Athletics* (A & C Black, 1990) for details of the technical components of running and hurdling. Because of the massive amount of work needing to be covered, athletes will have to make compromises in training based upon their

		100 metres	Long Jump	Shot Put	High Jump	400 metres
(a)	Performance needed to score:					
	1000 points	10.39 secs	7.76 m	18.40 m	2.21 m	46.17 secs
	750 points	11.51 secs	6.73 m	14.35 m	1.95 m	51.43 secs
	500 points	12.81 secs	5.59 m	10.24 m	1.65 m	57.57 secs
	250 points	14.46 secs	4.27 m	6.02 m	1.30 m	65.34 secs
(b)	Number of points gained by improvements of:	0.1 secs	10 cm	40 cm	5 cm	0.5 secs
At 1000 point standard		24	25	25	49	24
At 750 point standard		21	24	24	46	22
At 500 point standard		17	21	24	40	18
At 250 point standard		13	17	24	33	14

		Hurdles	Discus	Pole Vault	Javelin	1500 metres
(a)	Performance needed to score:					
	1000 points	13.80 secs	56.18 m	5.29 m	77.20 m	3 mins 53.79 secs
	750 points	15.85 secs	44.16 m	4.47 m	60.78 m	4 mins 29.25 secs
	500 points	18.25 secs	31.78 m	3.57 m	43.96 m	5 mins 10.73 secs
	250 points	21.36 secs	18.80 m	2.54 m	26.46 m	6 mins 03.62 secs
(b)	Number of points gained by improvements of:	0.2 secs	1 m	10 cm	2 m	2.5 secs
At 1000 point standard		27	21	31	31	19
At 750 point standard		23	20	30	30	16
At 500 point standard		19	19	26	29	14
At 250 point standard		13	18	22	28	10

Table 4 Shows (a) the performance required and (b) the number of points gained by improvements in decathlon at 1000, 750, 500 and 250 points standard

physical attributes, their skill levels, their weaker events, and the amount of time which they can afford to allocate to training.

'Playing the tables' is thus all part of the game. Working out where the most beneficial points gains can be made, and making these priorities in training, is part of the skill of the event. Those events from which the best points gains can be milked need to be identified, and have the largest proportion of winter training time allocated to them.

Even so, certain events can be considered as 'core' events. Once learned, high jump remains securely in the memory bank of the performer. It is thus good policy to spend time establishing this event early in the athlete's combined-event career.

Hurdling is common to both heptathlon and decathlon. The skill does not require great precision, but it does demand high levels of quite specific mobility and rapid repetition. High speed practice helps high speed running in general. For these reasons, the hurdles too is basic to combined events.

Shot put provides a sound base for each of the throwing events. Unlike men, many women do not take easily to the javelin. However, they cannot afford to squander valuable points by permitting it to remain a weakness.

The ability to pole vault is crucial to the decathlete. Without it he will never accumulate respectable scores.

Training

Table 5 outlines those qualities which all combined event athletes must work to enhance, and also indicates their relative importance to each individual discipline.

The most efficient way of bringing about improvement is by treating training as a 'whole', planning it so that maximum carry-over into related events is achieved.

The 1,500 metres is the most difficult running event to accommodate since it is half stamina and half speed. Most of its needs can be met by emphasising the speed and speed-endurance aspects of the 400 metres. This can be achieved through fast runs over 100 m to 300 m with very short rests, fast 'interval' runs over 200 m to 400 m with longer recovery and 30 to 40-minute runs daily or on alternate days. Such training will also cover most of the needs of the other running events, except for the 100 metres and the hurdles, for which 60 m flat-out runs, interspersed with a 4-minute recovery period, are more appropriate.

Speed is much affected by improvements in elastic strength, particularly of the leg muscles. Such work therefore must be part of the stock in trade of the combined eventer. Attention to leg and hip joint mobility is also vital, especially for hurdling, and will address most of the multi-eventer's needs below the waist. Additional work on the upper torso and shoulder girdle are necessary in order to cater adequately for the throwing events, particularly the javelin.

Table 6 outlines how training should progress from month to month throughout the year. For novices there should be greater emphasis upon training endurance and establishing skills at the beginning of the training year.

The most important adage relevant to combined event training is 'Strengthen the weak links without weakening your strengths'.

Competition

Accuracy and consistency are the hallmarks of a good combined events competitor. A fractional foul in long jump, or a long, flat javelin throw are of no value at all; with only three attempts available, such wasted efforts only contrive to place the performer under greater pressure. An overambitious choice of opening height in high jump or pole vault would be worse still.

It is vital, therefore, to select realistic opening jumps, and to make safe first attempts which are either well on to or even just behind the take-off board, or straight down the middle of the landing sector. Once a valid first effort has been recorded then it is possible to build upon it in subsequent attempts. Reserve inspired gambles for final efforts, when everything has gone well beforehand. They seldom succeed when you are off-form!

	Heptathlon	Decathlon
Speed	1. Hurdles 2. 200 metres 3. Long Jump 4. Shot Put 5. Javelin 6. High Jump 7. 800 Metres	1. 100 metres 2. Hurdles 3. Long Jump 4. Pole Vault 5. 400 metres 6. Shot Put 7. Discus 8. Javelin 9. High Jump 10. 1500 metres
Speed Endurance	1. 200 metres 2. 800 metres 3. Hurdles 4. Long Jump 5. High Jump	1. 400 metres 2. 1500 metres 3. Hurdles 4. 100 metres 5. Long Jump 6. Pole Vault 7. High Jump
General Endurance	1. 800 metres	1. 1500 metres 2. 400 metres
	As basic training for all other events	
Strength	1. Shot Put 2. Javelin 3. Long Jump 4. High Jump 5. Hurdles 6. 200 metres 7. 800 metres	1. Shot Put 2. Discus 3. Javelin 4. Pole Vault 5. Long Jump 6. High Jump 7. 100 metres 8. Hurdles 9. 400 metres 10. 1500 metres
Mobility	1. Hurdles 2. High Jump 3. Javelin 4. Shot Put 5. Long Jump 6. 200 metres 7. 800 metres	1. Hurdles 2. High Jump 3. Javelin 4. Discus 5. Shot Put 6. Pole Vault 7. Long Jump 8. 100 metres 9. 400 metres 10. 1500 metres
Rhythm	1. Hurdles 2. High Jump 3. Javelin	1. Hurdles 2. Pole Vault 3. High Jump 4. Discus 5. Javelin
	The remaining events all have some element of rhythm in their make-up	

Table 5 Performance factors in heptathlon/decathlon

October to December	January to March	March to April	May to September	October
Endurance	General strength	Special endurance	Speed endurance	Active rest
Skill	Stamina	Speed	Mobility	
Mobility	Speed endurance	Skill	Speed	
	Special strength	Special strength	Strength	
	Skill	Maximum strength		
	Mobility	Mobility		

Table 6

TRAINING

No one in their right mind would consider entering a test or an examination without first taking the trouble to prepare for it. In the same way, no athlete should consider entering a competition without first preparing for it thoroughly in training.

Training for athletics involves systematic preparation for competition. However, unlike academic preparation, which is all mental, athletic preparation must also be physical, with the physical aspect receiving most attention.

The central elements of training are speed, strength, stamina (endurance) and suppleness (mobility) which are all purely physical. These elements are allied to skill which is both physical and mental and because they all begin with the letter 'S' they are referred to as the five 'S' factors. They are all interrelated, and some possess several sub-elements. Strength, for example, has a number of different qualities. General strength is non-specific and relates to the all-round improvement of the strength levels of the whole athlete. Gross or maximum strength encourages the greatest expression of strength that a muscle can achieve. Elastic strength involves the expression of strength at speed and thus in its development loadings have to be lighter than for gross strength. Special strength is event-related, bringing about the optimum development of strength in those muscle groups directly involved in any particular event.

Similarly endurance can be allied to strength, and the whole matrix held together by skill and mobility, both of which have a limiting influence upon the other factors.

The importance which is assigned to each element varies according to each individual's age, physique, skill, experience and aims. Since it will also change according to the time of the year, it will, in fact, be changing constantly.

The coach, through his knowledge of the athlete and the principles of training, has to assess progress and to interpret training requirements so that movement towards improved levels of skill and fitness is never impaired. Good coaches get it right most of the time.

Table 7 shows an idealised representation of how training should be apportioned throughout the year for field event athletes.

Skill training

Field events have a very high skill requirement and at least two units of work (not to be confused with training sessions, since one training session may be composed of more than one unit of work) should be devoted to skill training each week. During the pre-competition and competition phases of training (see table 7) even more time can be devoted to skill refinement. Beginners, and those with technical defects, will need to devote more time to skill training especially during the early part of the training year.

During the early years of training it is important that attention is paid to those aspects of technique which are basic to the event. The establishment of a solid foundation paves the way for the finer points to be added at a later date. For this reason advice given at such times should be of the best quality, so that basic faults which are difficult to unlearn are avoided.

It will frequently be necessary to isolate portions of the complete skill, drilling them over and over again in order to perfect them. It will also be necessary to keep relating the portions to the whole, or total, skill. Great patience, even doggedness, is the key to becoming a successful field eventer.

	Oct	Nov	Dec	Jan	Feb	Mar	Apr	May	Jun	July	Aug	Sept
Phase of training	Preparation I			Preparation II			Phase 1	Competition	Phase 2		Phase 3	

JUMPERS

Weight training	Foundation Phase 50 per cent to 80 per cent 2xpw to 3xpw	Strength Gain 85 per cent to 100 per cent 3–4xpw	Power Phase 75 per cent Fast 3–2xpw	Strength Retention 1xpw at 90 per cent	R E
Special training	Endurance bounding	Power bounding	Jumping skill	Competitive jumping	S
Running training	300s and 200s plus some aerobic and general conditioning	200s get faster plus 100s and 40s		Sprinting mainly 40s and 60s plus some 100s	T

THROWERS

Weight training	Foundation Phase 50 per cent to 80 per cent 2xpw to 3xpw	Strength Gain 85 per cent to 105 per cent 3–4xpw	Power Phase 75 per cent Fast 3–2xpw	Strength Retention 1xpw at 90 per cent 1xpw at 75 per cent	R E
Special training	General training including circuits	Heavy implement throw plus end bounding	Skill plus Power bounding and light implement throwing	Competition skills—fast	S
Running training	Some aerobic running for 30–40 mins	150s and 100s	Sprinting 40 m and 50 m		T

Table 7 xpw=times per week

	Training effect	No. of Reps	No. of Sets	Recovery
100%	Maximum Strength	1–3	4–8	2–4 minutes
90%	General and Elastic Strength	6–8	3–4	1$\frac{1}{2}$–2 minutes
75%	Strength Endurance	8–15	3–4	45–90 seconds
55%	Speed endurance	10–15 against clock	3–6	45–90 seconds

Percentage of best single lift

Table 8   The specific effect of weight training loadings

101 and 102 Bounding exercises to develop speed

Because the level of concentration must be of a high order, any form of fatigue will disrupt skill learning. Short practice periods are therefore best, and 'little and often' is a sound principle to remember.

Speed training

Those field event athletes who need to be able to run quickly as part of their event follow a similar training routine to a sprinter.

However, the speed component in shot put or high jump is more obscure and thus more difficult to cater for. A more appropriate term for this component is impulse, since this denotes a force/time factor. The best way of improving this capacity is through fast, explosive activities.

In weight-training terms this means selecting lesser loads than one would use to develop gross strength, while ensuring that they are sufficiently high to employ the white twitch muscle fibres (i.e. between 75% and 85% of maximum). Exercises referred to as 'plyometric', or 'ballistic' are of this category. The bounding and throwing drills shown in table 9, and in photographs 101 and 102 typify such activities.

Although such training takes on special significance during the pre-competition portion of the training year, it is important that the 'feel' for speed is never lost but forms some part of the training regime all year round. Recent research indicates that ultimate speed (that which you will use when at the height of your powers) needs to be developed when still young. This is particularly true of throwers.

102

Strength training

Gross strength

Gross or maximum strength is best developed at loadings in excess of 90% of maximum. Maximum represents the greatest load which can be moved in one repetition, and it should be tested fairly frequently (e.g. monthly). For obvious reasons its cultivation involves neither speed nor endurance. It is necessary to the advancement of other, more specific aspects of strength and it is of great value to throwers.

Depending upon the actual weight lifted, athletes will only be able to lift the load a few times, perhaps one to three. They will then need to rest between sets (the technical term describing a block of lifts) for between two to four minutes. Such training is only necessary once per week.

Elastic and general strength

This type of lifting, using loads of between 75% and 90% of maximum, is the commonest. The difference between whether the effect is general or elastic lies partly in the loading, but mostly in the manner in which each lift is executed. Elastic strength involves the expression of strength at speed and so exercises need to be executed quickly and explosively if this component is to be trained. Loadings at the lighter end of the scale are most appropriate for this type of training.

For further advice on elastic strength training and appropriate exercises, refer to the speed training section of this chapter.

Strength endurance

Endurance is cultivated by doing an exercise many times. For this reason, light loads need to be used (see table 8).

Strength endurance is only required in limited amounts by field event athletes, although it does play an important role in the horizontal jumps and, in particular, the pole vault (see stamina section).

It is clearly very difficult to attempt 50 or 100 repetitions of a particular exercise without stopping, unless body-weight represents the only load. Usually, such totals are achieved by recourse to lifting in several blocks of 8 to 12 lifts (e.g. 5×10 reps $= 50$).

Multiple Jumps and Hops	'Depth' Jumping
1. Standing triple jump	1. From box rebound for height
2. Multiple hops over 25 m; 40 m; 60 m	2. Same as 1 but two-footed jump
3. Multple steps over 25 m; 40 m; 60 m	3. From box hop down and for distance
4. Multiple 2 hops and 2 steps over 25 m 40 m; 60 m	4. From box jump down and for distance
5. Timed 25 m hops	5. From box hop down and up on to second box
6. Timed 25 m steps	6. From box hop down and step on to another box before jumping off for distance
7. Multiple jumps up stairs	
8. Multiple jumps over hurdles (photograph 101)	7. From box hop down, step then jump over second box
9. Multiple hops up stairs	
10. Multiple hops over hurdles (photograph 102)	8. From box hop down, step then jump for distance

N.B. Boxes should be set ultimately at between 70 cm and 110 cm. Landings should where possible, be on to gymnastic mats to prevent injury.

Table 9   'Bounding' activities for developing elastic strength

There are several ways of grouping lifts in order to bring about specific training effects. Some of these are quite complex and time-consuming, and thus are more in the realm of the body-builder than that of the athlete, who has other training to do.

Systems of lifting

1. The simple set

3 sets of 6 reps at y load (kg or lb), usually written $3 \times 6 \times y$.

This represents the standard method of working. The load is advanced either by increasing the number of repetitions (e.g. from 6 to 7 to 8 or from 6 to 8 to 10, and so on), or by increasing the number of sets done. A simultaneous increase of both sets and repetitions is quite advanced and very stressful to the athlete.

An alternative method is to increase the load. This improves the quality of the work as opposed to the quantity which is advisable when commencing lifting or a new lifting year.

2. The pyramid

Set 1 – 6 reps at y	load (e.g. 45 kg or 100 lb)
Set 2 – 4 reps at $y+$	load (e.g. 55 kg or 120 lb)
Set 3 – 3 reps at $y++$	load (e.g. 61 kg or 135 lb)
Set 4 – 2 reps at $y+++$	load (e.g. 66 kg or 145 lb)
Set 5 – 1 rep at $y++++$	load (e.g. 68 kg or 150 lb)
Set 6 – repeated attempt at set 5 which may fail	

When set 6 is successfully completed it is a sign that all loadings can be increased.

The pyramid method is not very suitable for beginners because they should not train at maximum loadings for at least the first four months of lifting. Although it is a popular way of improving strength for experienced athletes, its great drawback is that it only subjects the musculature to one maximum stimulus per session. Multi-setting (i.e. doing several sets of one repetition) provides an alternative method of training which avoids this drawback.

The strength schedule

Muscles require between 24 and 48 hours in which to recover following hard work. Lifting on successive days is thus not advisable.

Top-class throwers will need to lift three, perhaps four, times per week throughout much of the training year. However, during the competitive season this will have to be reduced in order to permit fuller recovery. Jumpers and combined eventers will need slightly less, perhaps three sessions in mid winter, and only one or two during the competition season.

Combining exercises by alternating sets of one exercise with another which targets a completely different muscle group, offers a means of reducing the time that it takes to complete a lifting session. Since lifting can become quite time-consuming as it becomes more demanding, this is a sensible arrangement.

For advice concerning the selection of particular lifts you should consult a specialist book on strength training or weight-lifting, for example *Weight Training and Lifting* by John Lear (A & C Black, 1989) or *Conditioning for Sport* by Dr N. Whitehead (A & C Black, 1988).

Stamina

Field eventers need a degree of aerobic fitness in order to provide them with a sound physiological base for the specialist training they have to undergo. Many pundits argue the value of this type of fitness on the basis it helps to sustain an athlete throughout a long drawn out, six-effort competition, which may last some 90 minutes. There is no sound physiological basis for this viewpoint. What is required is the ability to sustain concentration, which is quite another matter. Aerobic fitness is required for the enhancement of the training regime, not the competitive one.

For the field eventer a reasonably frequent and regular 20 to 40-minute run will suffice.

This can be supplemented by circuit training which should be given some priority at the beginning of the training year; one unit per week should be adequate for the remainder of the year.

Suppleness

Reference has already been made to the need for athletes to work on mobility. This is particularly important in field events, for two main reasons. Firstly, in order to use their energies most effectively they have to apply them through as long a movement path as possible. Secondly, strength training, carried out over restricted ranges of movement, tends to bring in its wake restricted habitual length of the muscles concerned.

Improvements are brought about by learning to live with stretch in each of the joint complexes involved. The athlete should therefore seek 'outer range' positions in which the tendons and ligaments concerned are being stretched, and then learn to relax and hold that position while in some pain. The internal structures will then adapt and become 'happy' or comfortable in that state.

Vigorous bouncing or swinging exercises are not recommended. The use of partners who can gently pull and push the athlete into useful positions is to be encouraged.

Schedules

It is very difficult to lay down hard and fast rules. The level of skill of each athlete is a very individual thing, as are the physical and mental qualities.

In general terms, the training year should commence some seven or eight months before competition (October or November in the Northern Hemisphere), and follow a break taken after the previous season's competitions. At the beginning quantity should develop ahead of quality, so that it comes to a peak by the end of the first preparation period (table 7). However, quality should be in the ascendency during the second preparation period. The quantity of work should further diminish as competition draws near, while its quality should begin to approach that which will be demanded of the athlete during competition itself.

If training has been correctly planned and executed, it will produce a personal best for the athlete during the first phase of competition. This can be repeated during the third phase if both athlete and coach have been sensible, and have 'topped up' the system by reverting to the second type of preparation during the second phase of competition.

COMPETITION

Competition is the life-blood of athletics. It is the vehicle which facilitates evaluation of the success of training. Not to compete is not to be an athlete.

During the days preceding competition, a gradual reduction of the training load should be sought. If strenuous work has to be done it should be removed to the beginning of that week, as far from the competition as possible.

As the big day draws near thoughts of what is to come will start to crowd your mind. Make sure that those thoughts are positive and helpful. Create pictures of the perfect performance in your mind's eye, if possible at the venue itself.

Thoroughly plan the routine of the competition day. Work back from published event times and plan getting up in the morning, eating breakfast, travelling to the venue etc., giving yourself ample time for inspecting the ground, reporting to the officials and warming up after arrival. Try to anticipate any snags which could occur, and plan an alternative course of action. Make sure that all the equipment that you may need is in good order and packed. Keep a check-list for this purpose. Finally, focus your mind on success.

Warm-up

The pattern of the warm-up, and the amount of time needed to complete it, are very individual things. It is important to find a routine which suits you and to stick to it. However, the following guidelines may help.

1.   Raise your pulse rate to over 130 beats per minute. This can be done by jogging then slowly building speed through striding runs to fast runs.

2.   Intersperse this work with suppling exercises, paying particular attention to those joints or muscles which are going to be most used.

3.   Jumpers should measure out their approach runs either immediately before, or during their warm-up. They should be re-checked just before competition commences.

4.   Training drills should be used as part of the warm-up to create the best technical 'feel' of which the performer is capable. Once this has been established the athlete is ready to compete.

5.   The next step is to move away from other competitors, turn in on yourself and recreate those mental pictures of the perfect performance. Staying warm until the competition begins is also important at this time.

The use of practice throws or jumps is not advised, other than to get the feel of the circle or runway. They dissipate the nervous energy which has been accumulated, and which is essential to superlative performances.

Five minutes before the competition begins is not the time for perfecting technique. If this hasn't been accomplished during the months leading up to the event then it is already too late to put matters right.

The competition itself

If both long-term and pre-event preparation have been carried out correctly then this should be the moment you have been waiting for. Training should have shown that you were enjoying your best ever form and the build-up to the event should have stimulated you both physically and mentally. That being so, the first effort you make should be nothing less than your best ever. The rest is academic, for those particular conditions of preparation, confidence and anticipation can never be repeated, at least not until the beginning of another competition.

The frequency with which top performers actually do produce their best performance on their first attempt is quite uncanny. Bob Beamon's world shattering leap in the 1968 Olympic long jump final is just one outstanding example among many.

When following such a performance it is best for the competitor to put it immediately from his mind and to go on competing. Adversaries will respond and produce further challenges to be overcome, thus it is vital to remain alert and competitive right through to the end of the contest.

Vertical jumpers are presented with a slightly different challenge. Their best effort is not demanded until late in the competition, and they may not even start jumping until some time after others have begun. In some modern pole vault contests this may be hours after the start. Such athletes must learn to build gradually, for example by structuring the warm-up so that jumps taken at lower heights are in a sense a continuation of it. It is also possible to build one's mental approach so that it reaches a climax as the optimum height is reached. Most modern stadiums are constructed so that competition takes place under fairly consistent conditions. Competing in disadvantageous winds is now a relatively rare occurrence. Tail-winds are advantageous but they tend to push athletes towards take-off, making it necessary to lengthen the approach runs.

Approach runs also tend to become longer as the competition progresses, that is until the final two efforts when stress starts to take a hold and the run shortens. The clever athlete learns to adjust automatically for each anticipated eventuality.

Generally speaking, winds from the front right help discus throwers and javelin throwers. However, since the advent of the most recent design of javelin, tail-winds are now considered advantageous to the new implement. Tail-winds are also helpful to shot putters and hammer throwers because they blow them on to their heels and towards the direction of throw, assisting balance in the process.

Post-competition

It is important that the coach and the athlete come together to make a sober and reasoned assessment of the performance in the light of the preparation that preceded it. From this, further adjustments can be made which will be beneficial to those competitions to follow.

RULES

The International Amateur Athletic Board is responsible for regulating athletic competitions world wide and it frames the basic rules. National associations then modify these a little in order to make them applicable to special local conditions. Adoption of particular specifications for junior age groups provides a good example of such local deviation from the norm.

General competition rules

Field event competitors are permitted between three and six attempts, except in the vertical jumps. The exact form used will vary according to the nature and importance of the competition. In combined events it is always three, while in schools' competitions or at local club level, field eventers may well be limited to as few as three attempts. In more important competitions this will increase to six and follow one of the following patterns.

1. Three attempts, followed by three more for those placed highest at the end of the third round (this number varies according to the standard of the competition).
2. Up to three attempts (in a special qualifying competition) to reach a pre-set qualifying standard. Qualifying athletes then go forward to the competition proper, and are given further attempts by either of the mechanisms described in (1).

Each competitor is credited with the best of their attempts in the competition. In the case of a tie, the athlete achieving the better second best performance is awarded first place. If the result cannot be resolved despite all the efforts made, then the contestants 'jump-off', or 'throw-off' in order to produce a result.

Performances are measured from the inner edge of the rim or scratch line in throws, or the edge of the take-off board nearer the pit in jumps, up to the nearest mark made on landing. The tail of the javelin and the handle of the hammer are ignored for this purpose.

Athletes are permitted a set amount of time in which to make each attempt; $2\frac{1}{2}$ minutes for vault and $1\frac{1}{2}$ minutes for other events. They may stop and restart their attempt as many times as they wish within that time, provided that they do not infringe any other rules in doing so.

Horizontal jumps

Athletes are penalised if they:

■ touch the ground between the take-off board and the pit, except when executing the landing phases of the hop and step in triple jump
■ fall against the edge of the pit behind the point of landing
■ place check-marks on the runway
■ walk back through the pit after landing.

Vertical jumps

High jumpers and pole vaulters may jump above the minimum set for the competition, at any height which they choose, until they record three successive failures irrespective of height. They may thus elect to discontinue jumping at any height following a failure, and come back at a greater height. Failures at such heights are carried forwards and elimination takes place when these failures total three in succession.

A failure is recorded if they:

- dislodge the bar
- touch the ground, or landing area, beyond the plane of the uprights (or plane of the back of the box in pole vault), without clearing the bar.

High jumpers are not permitted to take off simultaneously from both feet, but they are allowed to use check-marks placed on the runway. Pole vaulters are not allowed to move the lower hand above the other after take-off, nor are they permitted to place check-marks on the runway. The pole is deemed to be part of the athlete in relation to the 'plane of the back of the box' rule, and it is considered a failure if they come back down on to the runway without having cleared the bar after take-off. Pole vaulters are permitted to adjust the uprights 40 cm towards them on the runway or 80 cm away from them and towards the landing area, using the back of the box as the datum line. They may use their own poles and they don't have to share them with other competitors.

Throws

Throwers may use their own implements provided that they have been submitted to the meeting referee for scrutiny, and that they are made available for use by other competitors. Hammer throwers may wear a protective glove on the hand which is in contact with the hammer, and shot putters are permitted to strap the wrist of their throwing hand. Elbow, knee and back supports are also allowed.

Touching the top of the circle rim, the stop-board or the scratch line is an infringement of the rules, as is leaving the delivery area before the implement has landed or leaving it from the front portion.

All implements must land within the inner edges of the lines marking out the landing sector.

Rules special to individual throwing events

Shot put

The shot must be kept in close proximity to the neck, and must stay ahead of the line of the shoulder.

Hammer

Hammer throwers may only stop a trial and start again provided that this is not as a result of the hammer-head hitting the ground. If this does occur, then the thrower may only stop if he keeps the hammer moving.

Javelin

Javelin has several very strange style rules. These state that:

- the implement must be held at the grip
- it must be thrown over the shoulder or the upper part of the throwing arm
- it must not be slung or hurled
- at no time during the throw may the thrower turn completely round so that the back is towards the landing sector.

As if these stipulations are not strict enough, the rules go on to say that non-orthodox styles are not permitted. This came about as the result of an inventive Spanish javelin thrower of the 1950s who devised a rotational style of throwing which launched the implement vast distances, but unfortunately put the lives of officials, fellow competitors and any spectators foolish enough to be around in great danger. He had to be stopped, and the current rules are the legacy of his initiative and originality.

CONVERSION TABLES

Imperial to Metric
(Key: 1 inch = 25.40 millimetres, 1 millimetre = 0.039 inches etc.)

Conversion formulae

To Convert	Multiply by	To Convert	Multiply by
Inches to Centimetres	2.5400	Ounces to Grams	28.3500
Centimetres to Inches	0.3937	Grams to Ounces	0.0352
Feet to Metres	0.3048	Pounds to Grams	453.6000
Metres to Feet	3.2810	Grams to Pounds	0.0022
Yards to Metres	0.9144	Pounds to Kilograms	0.4536
Metres to Yards	1.0940	Kilograms to Pounds	2.2050
Miles to Kilometres	1.6090	Tons to Kilograms	1016.0000
Kilometres to Miles	0.6214	Kilograms to Tons	0.0009

Inches		Millimetres	Feet		Metres
0.039	1	25.40	3.281	1	0.305
0.079	2	50.80	6.562	2	0.610
0.118	3	76.20	9.843	3	0.914
0.157	4	101.60	13.123	4	1.219
0.197	5	127.00	16.404	5	1.524

Yards		Metres	Miles		Kilometres
1.094	1	0.914	0.621	1	1.609
2.187	2	1.829	1.243	2	3.219
3.281	3	2.743	1.864	3	4.828
4.375	4	3.658	2.485	4	6.437
5.468	5	4.572	3.107	5	8.047

Ounces		Grams	Pounds		Kilograms
0.035	1	28.350	2.205	1	0.454
0.071	2	56.699	4.409	2	0.907
0.106	3	85.049	6.614	3	1.361
0.141	4	113.398	8.819	4	1.814
0.176	5	141.748	11.023	5	2.268

INFORMATION GLOSSARY

International Amateur Athletic Federation
3 Hans Crescent,
Knightsbridge,
London SW1X 0LN
Tel: 01 581 8771/2/3/4
Telex: 296859 IAAF HQ

The IAAF publishes much source material through the offices of its Development Commission. These include an excellent technical publication, *New Studies in Athletics*, published quarterly, a handbook (including rules), a quarterly bulletin, coaching posters covering every event, instructional videos covering all events and technical reports (including high quality biomechanical video) covering every major world championship competition since 1978. Publications order form and orders are available from the IAAF Publications Department at the above address.

Athletic Congress of the United States of America
PO Box 120
Indianapolis
Indiana 462060120
United States of America

British Amateur Athletic Board
Edgbaston House
3 Duchess Place
Hagley Road
Edgbaston
Birmingham B16 8NM
Tel: 021 456 4050
Telex: 334253 BAAB G

Sales/Publications Centre
5 Church Road
Great Bookham
Leatherhead
Surrey
Tel: 0372 52804

Through its Sales/Publications Centre in Surrey BAAB provide an excellent alternative English language coaching information service.

Publications include a quarterly coaching magazine, *Athletics Coach*, and instructional handbooks covering each event and special training elements such as mobility and strength. Coaching theory is addressed in manuals aimed at three different levels of experience, and teaching matters are covered in three booklets on running, jumping and throwing.

INDEX